DARKNESS TO LIGHT

"BUEN CAMINO"

DOUG ERICSON

The Pilgrimage of the Camino de Santiago-The Way.

The Camino de Santiago known as the Way of Saint James may be translated as a path or journey which is broader and much more expansive than any geographical track.The goal to walk 800km across Spain at first glance sounds rather unbelievable a task of endurance that only the most adventurous and inquisitive free spirited might undertake on foot.However,this traditional way from St-Jean-Pied-De-Port in France cross the Pyrenees to Santiago Spain has grown exponentially and has almost reached the status of a rite of passage for the young and for anyone beyond youth, a longing for direction,renewal and challenge,a longing for pilgrimage.
The Camino is different than any long distance bush trail which more often than not is taken as a wilderness experience,visiting remote and untouched vistas in search of primordial connection to creation and self.Whilst the Camino does pass though uninhabited wilderness,the way also traverses villages,towns and cities.The Camino is much more than a walk in the woods.

The Camino follows the pathway,historically reported as the journey taken by James,the patron saint of Spain who preached message of faith as a follower of Jesus,with particular emphasis on faith without works being dead or action in faith speaks louder than words.The association of James as the patron saint of Spain has no basis in the bible,but exists on the realm of tradition,oral history and myth.The event that catapulted the modest burial shrine of St.James as a place of pilgrimage was the battle of Clavijo in 852 were St.James was said to arrive on a white horse,holding aloft a fiery red sword,to assist the Christian army in fighting the Muslim invaders.This mythical act won him the name of St.James,the Moor slayer.The story mirrors the Muslim legends of Muhammad appearing in battle to assist the Muslim forces,who were said to carry relics of the Prophet.The Spanish in turn carried some ashes of the great warrior,St.James.The image of St.James was a convenient motif to draw Christian financial support to the frontier to assist the battle to maintain Christian domination of Spain.I suspect the Muslims had a similar objective in holding what was then a rich silver mining territory.

The peak of the Camino's attraction as a pilgrimage to follow James's pathway to his reported final burial home in the Santiago Cathedral was in the middle ages.In the 9th to 16th centuries ,up to two million people,or around 5000 pilgrims per day came to the burial place of St.James.The reformation in Europe and Spain's war with England saw the decline of Santiago as a place of pilgrimage in the 16th century. The Way is steeped in wars,with the march of Napoleon's army across the Pyrenees,the mythical stories surrounding the battle of Roland to advance of Charlemagne's army.

The many stories surrounding wars with the Muslims,stories of the Spanish warlord 'El Cid',the march of the Roman empire to as far back as Augustus Caesar and to the history of the Catholic church and the Jewish faith.All have nostalgia to any pilgrim on an adventure back in time and a touch of nostalgia in visual relics of the past in places of worship,museums and significant historic sights along the way.St.James,to the best of scholars seem to agree,never came to Spain. There is no earthly reason why his body should be brought to Spain and nothing is suggested in the Acts of the Apostles in the bible,where his death is recorded.He died several centuries before Islam was conceived,probably never mounted a horse in his life and certainly never slew an infidel.There is no earthly reason Santiago should be a place of pilgrimage, though it is.

The revival of the route we call the French Way was a vision of Don Elias(1929-1962). He documents,articles and a thesis on the Camino for the university of Salamanca. He was convinced of the importance of the ancient trail and set himself the challenge of reviving the route.In 1984 he put into motion his mission to rescue,clean and mark the trails along the Camino.He also started marking the iconic yellow arrows to indicate the right way at very tricky crossroads along the trail.

He started an association and created groups to maintain the arrowed route of the Camino.He also travelled throughout European universities and attended meetings explaining the importance of the Camino de Santiago as a place of communication and understanding for people of all nations.We probably owe him the fact that the Camino is still in existence at all! Santiago,once more grew in importance in 1989 when Pope John Paul 11 visited the Cathedral and in 1993,a holy year,the entire French route was added to the UNESCO World Heritage site list.From then on, interest in the Camino exploded,with hundreds of pilgrim accommodations began springing up and an increase in practical resources produced by regional tourism bureaus as well as independent authors,helped the cause.

Modern day pilgrims walk the Camino Way for their own reasons which may be to do with the past,the present and maybe even the future.Some take the way as just a long walk or just to improve their health.Still others may venture forth because they like the idea of moving from one place to another.Some are on the pilgrimage to pursue a spiritual quest,to figure something out in a discerning way,to seek guidance from a power greater than self or just find a way of letting go the thoughts of the head,taking a deep breath ,smell the variety of odours,let the feet do the walking and just see what comes up.Everybody has their own reasons for doing the Camino de Santiago.

CONTENT

A Dedication to My Children

..... for Scott, Sam and Emma
and the memory of Peter.

The Mythical journey and the Legends of the Teller

"There are depth of love that I cannot know,
till I cross the narrow sea,
There are lights of joy that I may not rest,
till I rest in peace with thee"

-Fanny Crosby,American hymn writer.

The fundamentals of life's experiences,regardless of the nature of our background is embedded from our parents,childhood experiences,family life and the journey we have along the way. Mother Earth and Father Sky are the great mythical symbols of the origin of our world as well as our own beginnings.We have all come from somewhere and whatever we make of ourselves late in life,we cannot undo the past.We inherit the genetic and psychological patterns of our family background and through our numbered days upon this earth,we become partly our own creation and partly the legacy of the past.

The journey of my Camino is a journey of my life's experiences through joy,pain,suffering and a letting go of past through poetic expression.The Camino caused me to be reborn into some kind of renewal of faith in my ability to create,touched by the hand of the great poetic Master who led my hand to express poems and songs of the life I now know in writing this book.The myths I had lived by,the people I met along the way ,my dreams and aspirations for the future, are all expressed here. It was not my intention to write of these things for I had no specific goal in doing the Camino,but to come to terms with inner conflict and perhaps see a mission statement it would have read "a spiritual journey" but instead it became for me a journey of the spirit,my spirit!

It is coincidental that the poetry herein is written in eight sections as is the journey broken up into eight sections from St-Jean- pied-de-port to Santiago.Travel agents sell the journey in eight sections and pilgrims tend to do a section at a time,returning every year to do yet another section until the journey is completed.Indeed many return every year to do the Camino all over again.Hiking guidebooks tend to break the 800 kilometres walk into similar sections.My epic journey to do the whole distance in one go was partly influenced by the fact that we down under have a long way to travel to the northern hemisphere and the fact that I believed I was on a journey of the spirit as each step brought me closer to letting go and renewal.The purpose of this book is to share with you factual and mythical stories and imagery,bringing relief from internal conflict and help both you,dear reader, and me to discover greater depth,richness and meaning in life.

You may wish to refer to my website www.caminoway.com.au,check out what I have to offer in the future,join the pilgrim community by writing on my blog or simply write to me pilgrim@caminoway.com.au,if you consider you wish to do a Camino or simply be a part of my life and my community.Through the darkest hours of my existence I learnt though suffering,loneliness and failure,to discover new light and new hope through doing the Camino de Santiago.I trust you gain in some small way ,a benefit from reading this book, if it be in a poem or just a word that inspires you to new myths,legends and a better future for you,then this book has been worthwhile.

"Buen Camino"

Doug Ericson

OPENING CHAPTER

"The Spiritual Awakening"

WWW.CAMINOWAY.COM.AU

The spiritual awakening

It was not just the songs that he longed to sing,not the poetry that he found in expression but the poetry of his heart that cried out for life. He had come to a mystical side of himself that could not be expressed in words or worldly deeds .A cause that could only be fulfilled by the spirit that was central to the candle that burnt within.

A candle that was to him a symbol of life itself,a flame that burnt at a deep level,projecting light into darkness and in the flickering awareness he could almost hear its message "exist-stay alive-survive."He heard the words of Lao Tzu, the 460 B.C. Chinese philosopher that had come to him from words of some modern sage, although he himself had not read Lao Tzu, the words rang deep within him "In breathing stillness of body and mind, an inner flame is born."

Whilst his own body coiled tightly with anxiety and the panic state that comes from clutching too tight a hold on himself as his worldly claims engulfed him. He was learning about himself for the first time,aware of his body, his mind and the true spirit within him. Learning in his current aloofness, that running around the pit of inner hell he had created for himself had only caused greater anxiety and he was now completely exhausted. He did not have the strength or bodily health at this time to endure a short walk let alone consider climbing great mountain ranges of which he often dreamed.

Here he sat rugged up in the comfort of four walls and a heater when he would much prefer being snug in his knapsack on some magic mountain or lonely plain, sharing his lot with his higher power or a lover.Yet here he was surrendering his ego, free falling moment to moment to moment into that surrendering and taking the risk to free fall into the unknown.The fearful dragons mouth of self acceptance, the fear of falling down into a pit of darkness where the dragon lived ,where there was no light only darkness,of weeping and gnashing of teeth.

He had fallen part of the way before, when he lost all that he thought his life was about.Wife,children, friends,business and wealth, had left him and it was then that he turned to other lovers. Lovers who had brought him their pain in his pain, comfort in his agony, ego illusion in their mystic love rites,a sense of the goddess for a brief moment only to find disenchantment and once more illusion. A cover of the inner truth that he was seeing clearly for the first time in his life.

He had turned to regain the respect of his children only to find that they had moved on as was their right and all he could do was be there in the event of their fall, be there now in a sober mind. If nothing else, this was the greatest lesson he could teach them. He would continue to remain sober a day at a time. He had struggled to regain the wealth that he once possessed only to find that in time apart from the need of food, clothing and shelter and essential services, the pursuit of wealth was of little comfort in a modern world of which he was no longer a part.The lessons once more done, he realised that the ways of the past no longer held weight with him and his heart no longer craved what was once his sure fire way to enthusiasm for living.

So now he visualised his physical self as the coiled spring and in its inner core a golden spiritual thread that was empowered through the centre of the earth, through the centre of his being to the heavens above and beyond into the universe. A golden light of energy that tapped into the core of God, to himself, to the earth and in turn to every living thing that attuned to its likeness.

He had taken an inner truth of honesty to himself, of open mindedness and a willingness to grow. A willingness not to worry, of acceptance ,of belief in courageous opportunity to live in a continuum of momentous spiritual awareness. Just to live with whatever came up.He began to relax now to allow the coil of wound up spring to slowly unwind, let go and trust God without definition.

In his acceptance he came to realise, in the inner core of his being that he was truly a loner and outsider, as it is (in heaven) from the inside out ,a true free spirit of his age. Numerically he belonged to 2%-3% of the population of the earth's people, that three in every hundred who did not belong in the bubble of life. He realised that the bulk of humanity were square pegs trying to fit into round holes and it was madness,a madness that he had become party to for the bulk of his lifetime and he was sad that it took so long for his awakening.

This was to him an enormous discovery and it was taking time to sink in. That through the passage of time he, like the small percentage of his fellow voyagers, truly accept we are born outsiders, genetically blue printed to be as we are. This in time, he now knew would bring great peace and hope for the future and he knew he had to let it sink into the marrow of his bones.The synchronicity, meaningful co-incidences of his true journey was at its dawning and the spiritual core of his inner being danced.

He knew it was not the old ways of his strength, enthusiasm, leadership and dogma that would project him like an arrow to some designated target. Rather,
it was to be a slow road ,one day at a time, moment to moment to moment, using the spiritual thread of the coiled spring to unwind, unravelling and letting go to an inner calm.

He was learning to use no force now, to let the force within take hold;allowing time to heal and the energy grow. He knew that he needed to go with the grain in the wood as any artist in timber knows. Often in the past he had to run against the grain and the result was splinter wounds.Yes, he was now running with the river of life, going with the flow and he had put his boat of personality into the inner river of life and was going with the current in open water. He knew once he got the drift of it, it was just a matter of a gentle movement of the rudder.

It was time to surrender and let it soak into the marrow of his bones.He knew once more he was coming to a vacuum and it was time once more to free fall into the pit,into the bottomless pit where the dragon lived.He knew once he descended into the dragon's mouth in his mind, that there he would find a lotus flower.
There,free falling into the hell of the bottomless pit,he would reach a vacuum of nothingness. "No-thing-ness". There the dragon would turn into a lotus flower of creative ideas which is the womb of rebirth.

On his previous fall into the pit he had taken a parachute of meaningless clutched possessions and wild ego notions,a crutch to lessen the fall and the residual inner nervous tension remained,So this time he was going all the way without a parachute, without forethought, without a plan.

We surrender to win!
We give way to keep!
We suffer to get well!
We die to live!

He was learning the way as the middle road. He concluded that the way could not be achieved by linear, rational, sequential, logical means. He knew these ways as being half brained notions of a world external to his being.He knew now of the third way, the way of his spirit and his imagination.

A way tempered by the boat of his personality floating on the water of life, adjusting the rudder of existence ever so slightly from within his spiritual core. He was now on a new quest and had joined the seekers of the inner truth which becomes the universal truth. He knew in his quest, that like his outward expression of tramping some bush track he had to be aware of danger of nature being both cruel and kind.

As a seeker of inner truth he was on dangerous ground in a world of material madness and chaos. He needed to be as vigilant as a female serpent and innocent as a dove. He would carry with him forever more the inner sword of discernment, that perfect right of freedom of choice.

"We ought not to live the afternoon of our life the way we have lived out the morning of our lives" Yung.

So the new life of the inner spiritual journey was unfolding. He was still in between the old way and the new, but he was learning to let go and let that inner core of being take hold that something from nothingness. that nothing (no- thing- ness) where he now believed the universe began, where something came from nothing,was his God.He discovered within himself a way of cutting through to the reality of everything that made up his life. He discovered within himself an enlightened ability to judge and act with wisdom. He discovered symbolically a sword of discernment, a tool to carry as his staff of action, his brand of reason.

He had a choice now, to use a Sword of Discernment, like a knight of old, to just go with the flow, nice and easy and accept whatever comes up with free will.To use a sword of discernment with wisdom and understanding when and where he may think fit. To pursue or not to pursue in consideration of who and what he was becoming and as he was becoming to realise he always was, is and will be. His right to act or not to act according to the dictates of his conscious, his heart and the beauty that lived within him and every human being with whom he would now come in contact on his outward and inward journey.

A journey of understanding, a journey of nature being both cruel and kind,of being vigilant as a female serpent within his inner being on the pathways of his life and innocent as a dove.A freedom nothing bar death could take from him, his freedom of choice for living.He knew within his heart of hearts there lived a Sword of discernment and he longed for an outward expressive symbol of his inner need and courage. He would venture forth to let go of his inner turmoil. Take a journey of the spirit, his spiritual heart expressed in a real symbol.He could think of no better way than the way of St James ,the apostle whose symbol was a real Sword of Discernment .The sacrificial cross of St James, a floury Fitch, where the sword blade makes it a sword of a warrior.

He would follow the path of St James on the Camino way, where he would lay down his inner burdens; walk the traditional way that so many pilgrims had walked before him. He knew now the outward expression would manifest into the sword of discernment of St James.Like the Spanish conquerors who fought and won their war against the Moors so many centuries ago.

Their vision of the saint on a white steed advancing before them with the red sword of Santiago leading the charge.He would venture forth on the road to Santiago,leading ever onward in a courageous cry to the quest that pierced his heart.He would walk the Camino de Santiago!

He knew that his outward Sword of Discernment would be the pen and not the sword.He would express in words the cry of his heart,the link he had to his past journey,his current turmoil and his spiritual quest.He would venture forth with hope and confidence,despite the dark night of the soul.The thought of a new dawning from the dark night gave him courage to step forth.The night is darkest just before the dawning and despite the sword that pierced his soul,he ventured forth.

When we no longer know where
to turn the journey has just begun

The pathway of the dream.

Some men walk a lonely path,
just to keep the flame alive,
like some messenger,
with a torch,
holding the flame on high!

Dreams are just some myth,
in the colours of the mind,
well worn like some faded cloth,
a flag we wave with pride,
like some moth to a flame!

Now I don't know
when the dream faded,
the pattern changed the shape,
the old dream just died,
and a new one took shape.

Life is mostly froth and bubble,
the epitaphs carved in stone,
dreams are passing fantasy,
so be kind to those in trouble,
take courage in your own!

The queen of hearts sits alone,
holding my heart in her hand,
pondering the consequences
of holding on,
or just letting go!

Oh! I have so many choices,
ten of Wand is the card I hold,
maybe I am out of aces,
on this pathway,
on my way home!

The hangman's contemplating,
the feelings of this space,
the choices of the reasons,
in seasons of the heart,
is it time to make a start!

Life is mostly froth and bubble,
the epitaphs carved in stone,
dreams are passing fantasy,
so be kind to those in trouble,
take courage in your own!

Time is just a pathway
for the Page of the wands,
making choice of the dream,
to hold on too,
winding my way back home!

The horizons may be plenty,
making ones choice in the rhyme,
letting go of the old ways,
many dreams to carry on,
doing just one at a time!

Now I am sitting on a mountain,
the view is looking fine,
ten thousands loyal virgins,
seated at my side,
as the light fades in my mind!

Life is mostly froth and bubble,
the epitaphs carved in stone,
dreams are passing fantasy,
so be kind to those in trouble,
take courage in your own!

Watching a new sunrise,
in the windows of the mind,
letting go the tarot readings,
holding four aces in hand,
living this day at a time!

Some men walk a lonely path,
in the shadows of the mind,
then the days come dawning,
leaving the past behind!
living with a straight flush now!

Section 1-St-Jean-Pied-de-Port to Pamplona.

The ascent of the Pyrenees to the famous Roncesvalles pass is probably the most difficult of the whole of the French way to Santiago.The 'Napoleon Route' starts with a steep climb past country houses before reaching mountain meadows,the cross, which is the first pause for letting go burdens.The Camino changes to sweeping spectacular mountain views merging into woodlands towards the French/Spanish boarder and descends to Roncesvalles.

From Roncesvalles,The Camino de Santiago trail continues through beech and oak woodlands,crosses two mountain passes before descending towards Zubrini,across across the medieval Rabies Bridge and over the river to Arga.

The Camino follows the river to Larrasoana,an important stop for pilgrims in medieval times.The journey towards the famous city of Pamplona gets busy with pilgrims as it has done historically.Famous for its running of the bulls,San Fermin festival,the city of Pamplona attracts pilgrims to its medieval streets,cathedral,famous local food and wine and favourite coffee houses and haunts of the writer of the running of the bulls, Ernest Hemingway.

" When we no longer know where to turn the journey has just begun. "

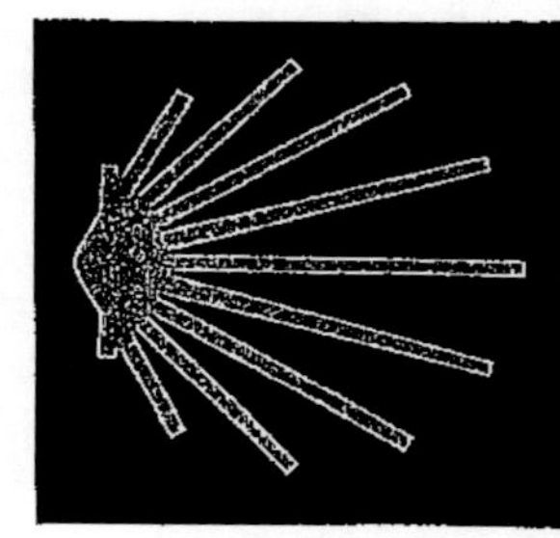

SECTION 1-ENTERING THE DRAGON'S MOUTH

THE DARKNESS

Somewhere before dawn

Here I am in my empty room,
alone with my exhausted thoughts,
of shattered dreams and yesterdays.

A hollow vessel without sound,
a shell on a deserted beach,
cast out of the sea of life.

A shell etched with the lines,
a road map of a past life,
no longer knowing that existence.

A hollow vessel with out sound,
a shell on a deserted beach,
cast out of the sea of life.

A shell that once was part,
of natures living organism,
but no longer of such use.

Once a vibrant living part,
of Gods unfathomed nature,
no longer in the circle of life!

A hollow vessel without sound,
a shell on a deserted beach,
cast out of the sea of life.

Yet such a shell has destiny,
it has its part to play,
to turn from shell to sand!

Sand on a deserted beach,
it's beauty can be grand,
It's part of life's great circle,
brings rebirth to a shell.

Yet here I am in my mind,
on a deserted beach,
in my empty room,
looking back along the beach,
there are no footprints,
not even my own.

Washed away by the tide,
I cried!
and wonder why did I not take
the high ground,the sand hills
safe from the rolling tide,
I cried,

And looking back I see,
a hollow vessel without sound,
a shell on a deserted beach,
cast out if the sea of life.

No footsteps ahead,
no foot prints behind,
those cast,
washed away by the tide.

I trudge on ,
for I cannot hide,
trusting in God's nature,
seeking a new path of the mind,
looking for higher ground.

Contemplating the spirit,
of my inner child,
climbing now a different path,
clinging to life and love.

Hearing the sounds of the sand,
under my feet,
knowing the purpose of a shell,
renewed in a creative grace,
we sift life.

Looking to the higher ground,
the spirit of my childhood ,
seeking to leave footprints,
for some future purpose.

So I will climb a different pathway,
leave the sand and sea behind,
awaken to the spirit,
new vision in my mind.

Peter.

We had a son his name was Peter,
was the pride of family,
somehow he became the rock,
the knead that held our clay.

Every kingdom needs a jester,
he was ours,'twas plain to see,
he was always up to mischief,
playing jokes on all he'd see.

True at heart he was a bush boy,
shooting slugs to kill a rat,
riding motor bikes in round up,
climbing trees and all of that!

Loved his model train when raining,
liked to watch an eagle fly,
hear the sound of pine trees falling,
with a gleeful sparkling eye.

Loved to ride his Yamaha,
with its great big black exhaust,
got his kicks with pro linked suspension,
and low handle bars of course!

He'd speak of chicken cooking,
and the smell of country air,
of the laughter of some people
and the roses he smelt there!

Loved to feed small pigs when snorting,
hear the thump of rabbits foot,
watched for hours small birds flying,
climbing trees and cutting wood!

When we moved into the city,
loved to play his rugby game,
didn't like the thought of losing,
took great relish in the fame!

As he grew he was a dresser,
wearing his Tag Heuer watch,
always dressed in Ralph Lauren,
Nike Airs his brand of course!

and a reverse hat upon his head,
like we see when Lleyton wins!

He found joy in Christmas paper,
and the lights of the Christmas tree,
loved to give and watch the smiles,
in gift giving family.

Just a boy who loved the world,
all that gathered there within,
through the light of his great spirit,
a darkness was creeping in.

So he drove himself in work life,
and he climbed a corporate tree,
but not before he set up business,
with me and the family.

When the darkness in his mindset,
began to take a hold,
took a job in west New Guinea,
were he found a pot of gold!

He got jilted by a lover,
falsely diagnosed as ill,
began to doubt the life he lived,
stopped taking depression pills.

It was then the rot set in,
he decided to let go,
so with noted pen on paper,
he said good bye ,
and he just packed it in.

When the sun set on Santorini,
and the Greeks just take it in,
I remember what he said,
it was the happiest he'd been.

Sometimes when I see a bird fly,
I can't help but think of him,
walking hand in hand together,
we where both little boys back then!

Yes,he cut his fair share of life,
and he roared like a meteor,
across the skies of his perception,
but he burnt out in the end.

Now I miss his smiling face,
and his devotion to family,
feel the sadness that I know,
of the pains without relief,
we his blood are so grief stricken,
God in heaven give us peace!

There is a cockatoo that's flying,
In the shadow land of heart,
across the great Australian landscape,
on the other side of dark.

Yes,it's flight is toward the dawning,
where it will cry to morning sun,
telling all of natures glory,
of a suicidal son.

It's time to let him go now,
may your boy's soul rest in peace,
whilst those of us still living,
do our best to find release.

Sing

"We shall over come,
We shall overcome
We shall overcome
Some day,

Oh!deep on my heart,
I do believe,
We shall overcome'
some day."

" Not I... or anyone else, can travel that road for you,
you must travel it yourself"

- Walt Whitman.

The inner man,

Well I met the sage,
in a cage,
in the corners of my mind,
we travelled near,
I travelled far,
searching for a truth!

In this painful tale,
over hill and dale,
he helped me seek the truth,
it is in things beyond the mind,
in my eternal youth!

So turn the pages of the mind,
seek and you shall find,
the answer to life's riddle,
hand to the grindstone
morning glory,

in search of the holy grail.

The message is clear,
let go of this madding quest,
for life you will then find,
take nothing for your journey,
just your state of mind.

An hour has passed,
the sage now moves,
bids me farewell independent inside,
with a parting sound I am hearing
"Enter your thoughtful cell!"

"The hour is darkest just before the dawn"

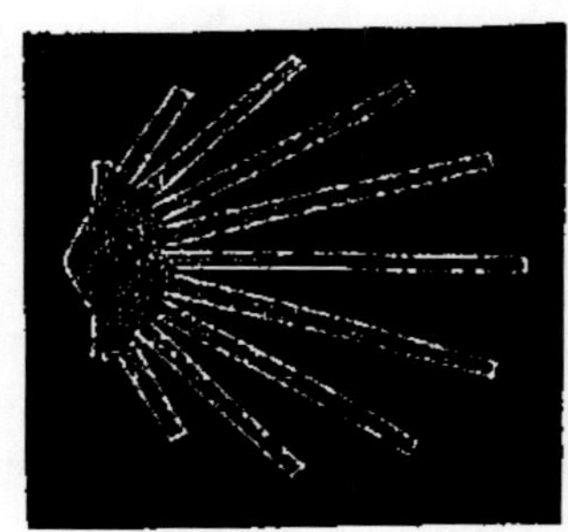

He'll roll you over jack!

There are millions and millions
of steeples ,
counting the big and the small,
all of them point up to heaven,
saying there's room for all,

There's a gate to that
heavenly kingdom,
and the key to that gate
is a prayer,
and no one is questioned
nor humbled,
in spite of the cross they bear.

Big change is a coming,
It's Roll'n down the track,
big change is a coming,
It's Roll'n down the track,
better get a move on,
It'll roll you over jack!

My love is a soulmate,
her spirit is intact,
my earth soul is a lover,
she's waiting on her back,
better get a move on
she'll roll you over jack!

The spirit is a coming,
he's roll'n down the track,
the spirit is a coming,
he's roll'n down the track,
better change your way now,
he'll roll you over jack!

"Give me that old time religion,
give me that old time religion,
give me that old time religion,
it's good enough for me!"

Jesus is a soul-man,
he's roll'n down the track,
Jesus is a soul-man,
he's a monkey on your back,
better get a move on
he'll roll you over jack!

Our world is a changing,
It's roll'n down the track,
our world is a changing,
It's roll'n down the track,
pace set for disaster,
it will roll you over jack!

The new world is awakening,
there's no time for turning back,
the new world is awakening,
embrace this loving fact,
reach for the highest star now,
It'll roll you over jack!

"Give me that old time religion,
give me that old time religion,
give me that old time religion,
it's good enough for me!"

Battered old warrior

A warrior brave,
driven by ego need,
stepped out in his smart steel armour,
fancy sword and fine bright shield.

Steadfast he proclaimed his talents ten,
tested his metal and won,
returning on his golden stead,
for victory laurels he had some,
egged on by the masses of men.

The ceremonies continued,
for a brave and chosen one,
praises from the masses,
as all cheered him on,
glory hunters and next of kin.

A warrior broken,
driven by fear,
no one for his armoured cause,
no fancy sword
and fine bright shield.

A warrior broken,
hiding in shadows,
shirking his talents ten,
wounded heart driven by fame and fortune,
no glory hunters or next of kin.

A battered old warrior,
strengthened by his inner God,
adventures in friendship,
compassion and prayer,
forgiving himself and his kin,

He's a battered old warrior,
world weary driven by God,
quietly learning to share,
the spoils of his talents,
be they one,five or ten.

New servant to the pathway,
no loner for a course,
he a real Don Quixote,
fighting a heavenly quest.

OH! SARAH,SARAH

"Oh! Sarah,Sarah,where are you now,
in the spirit world beyond?
the first sign of father daughter love,
as the star filled rays did come.

Oh! Sarah,Sarah,the light of peace,
cast down on daughter and son,
your birth was death,
death brought light,
as star filled rays did come.

Oh! Sarah,Sarah,celestial love,
took away the pain,
of a mother and father,
who trust in peace,
we may see your face again."

Seeded Dawn

Great blobs of fiery sunlight,
breaks the surface of unfathomed darkness,
rippling through the leafy stillness,
reality dawns on blinking eyes.

streaming light fills former blindness,
a new awakening measures skies illumination,
the source sun appears flinging warmth to fragile earth,
creations diamond magic dewdrops on the landscape.

The almighty beam of oceanic light,
tiptoes across the dawn,
as the last shadows of the darkness,
fold back into the void.

Light penetrates the dreamtime,
heralding a new beginning,
of natural love embrace,
in the beauty of the immeasurable sun.

In an energy of universal clarity,
the sunlight shapes the dawn,
boldly holding back the cause,
of shadow,wind and rain.

In the midst of this greater glory,
in the arms of an in depth love,
a new Adam embraces the beauty,
in a new seeded dawn love!

"Hope is a waking dream"

- Aristotle.

" Yes,there is a Nivanah, it is in leading your sheep
to a green pasture, and in putting your child asleep
and in writing the last line of your poem.

- Kahill Gibran.

The end of the rainbow

The sun's rays flash dark curtains open,
fiery eyes herald the sun,
morning star on fading moon drops,
rain in mystic colours run,
directing dreamers to their gold,
somewhere beyond the rainbows beam,

Stumbling dreamers,leading souls;
turning back from clouded night,
in your age of youth and wisdom,
you seek strength,both brave and bold.

When your body loses strength,
you are overcome by fear,
life's boldness no longer beckons,
for in truth you're growing old,

Yet you seek the seed of wonder,
from beneath the rainbow's gold,
chains are breaking,freedom's dawning,
as you tramp the mountain's path,

Climb the highest peak you can find,
stumbling down the vale below,
the pot of gold keeps on moving,
as a new rainbow unfolds.

Seek your God in desolate places,
that's what only we fools do,
stay a while in spirit stillness,
the pot of gold inside of you!

“The traveller,the pilgrim,cannot find deep meaning in their journey until they encounter what is truly sacred.”

- Phil Cousineau

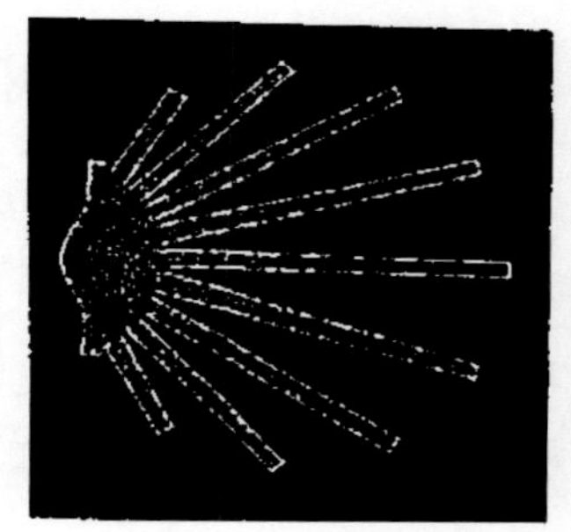

Taken on by the light

There are tracks where I must travel,
pathways of the spirit,
only God knows and little children
of the kingdom of heaven.

In the passing of time,
so much has been lost,
in sadness and shadow,
we carry our cross.

Forgive and forget now,
just move right along,
now is the moment,
just walk in your song,
ascend God source light,
lead on.

Keep our feet
on the pathway of love,
Christ in presence,
let go,let love.

It's never too late
let go of fear,
walk in the springtime,
of laughter and tear.

Pause in the life stream,
stepping out there,
live in the moment,
bring our worlds together,
say a little prayer.

" Write it in your heart that every day is the best day of the year. "

- Ralph Waldo Emerson.

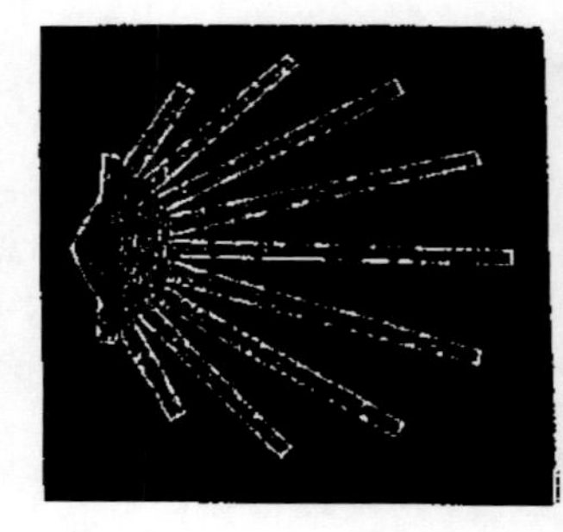

Soul shattered miracle

We are but shattered pieces,
of a mirror in the void,
a universal reflection,
of the light in the darkest scene.

A mirror of a prism,
beaming visions of illumination,
a dull reflection of the glory,
in thought,in word ,in deed,

The great awakening of the cosmos,
as in chaos it evolves,
to some orderly existence,
in a sound that we don't know.

Man cannot recreate,
the mirror of creation,
but we can conceive,
some order out of chaos!

This godly world's a miracle,
a dream beyond belief,
in unity of purpose,
all things are possible.

In a one world united,
where love rains hate is dead,
the world's wounds can be mended,
so let the miracle begin.

This godly world's a miracle,
as oneness we are God,
in unity of purpose,
all things are possible!

"The search is what anyone would want to undertake if he/she were not sunk in the everydayness of his or her own life.....to become aware of the possibility of the search is to be on to something.Not to be on to something is to despair."

-Walker Percy,the moviegoer.

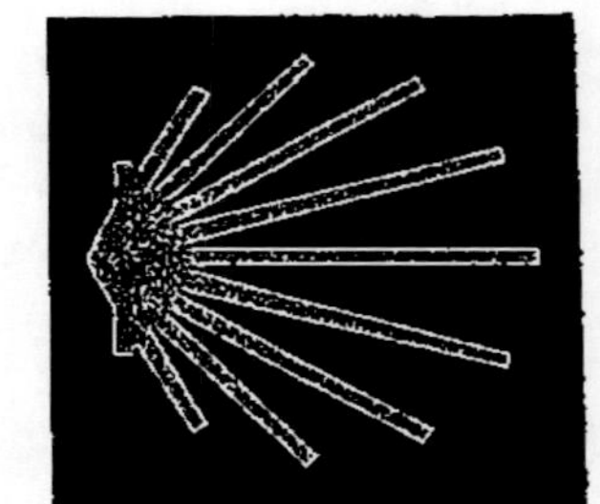

"Faith is the bird........"

There was once a broken little bird
who lost the gift of flight,
or so it seemed in its darkest hour,
the wind was not quite right,

How could the air in storm or mist
help a bird to flight?
how could he sing to other birds,
for there was none in sight?

So there he was alone and lost
in sadness and in doubt,
it was to this little bird,
what life was all about.

Going deep within its agony,
our feathered friend rehearsed,
searching down memory lane,
praying not to be bound to earth,
was he not made to fly and soar,
why was it in reverse?

To search to chance some carefree way,
to jump and trust to fly,
our bird searched for an easy route,
so that this bird might fly.

But in the scary moments,
the unbelief prevailed,
so he began to doubt the truth
for flight to bird was fable!

In time of course the renewed bird,
believed he was all right,
climbed to the highest mountain top,
there to attempt to flight.

So with courage before reason,
he jumped from this great height,
and with the help of wind and air,
this bird returned to flight,

Footnote:
"Faith is the bird that feels the height
and sings while the dawn's still dark."
- Lagore.

CRAB APPLE TREE

In the middle of my good friends garden is a crab apple tree and being winter,it has lost all its leaves. The garden surrounding this tree is a most beautiful array of green hedges and delicate evergreens and perennials that have retained their green leaves,awaiting for the springtime of buds and flowers.You see my friend is an artist who does horticulture for a living and gave up painting pictures to create this world of beauty right in her own back yard.She has a passion for gardening and no effort is to strenuous for her, when it comes to her garden,it's her hearts passion.

Now,I know nothing about gardening nor the names of plants in english much less their latin names,and whilst I recognise the beauty I behold in her backyard,I somehow resonate with the crab apple more than any plant.

The crab apple being a deciduous tree has loss it's leaves and stands awkward and rather skeleton like in its nakedness.

Like the crab apple loosing its leaves,I have shed many a layer of my outer shell in recent times due to mayor natural and unnatural events in my life.This sometimes causes me to be raw and awkward in my coming to terms with life,as slowly more of me is exposed to nature and who I am.It also has the effect,particularly on cloudy cold days or when I am feeling unwell,to send me into a desolate lonely place in my inner cell that I sometimes feel,in the depth of despair and that I will never rise above.

It is then that I take heart from the crab apple tree,even though it appears raw and awkward in its nakedness,standing alone in a garden of green,it somehow give me strength and courage to face up to life.

Already the crab apple tree has small buds awaiting the coming spring,even though it has the appearance of a cold unloved emptiness.

I must say that I cannot remember what the crab apple trees flower looks like and in the past did not really care.However,now that I am in the winter of my own fragility,irritability and discontent,I am looking forward to the crab apple in flower in the coming spring.

The hour is always darkest just before the dawn and I feel sure,if I wait patiently,despite my current nature and life circumstance,I trust that I too ,like the crab apple tree,will bud again and flower in the spring.

Section 2-Pamplona to Logrono

As Pamplona fades into behind,the pilgrim begins the long ascent to the 'hill of forgiveness' where the pilgrim sculpture at the 'alto' is a timely reminder of the thousands who walked this path for over centuries.The 360 panoramic views of Pamplona and the valley ahead is a site to behold.The descent to Puente la Reina(Queen's Bridge) and its medieval alleys and the impressive eleventh century bridge leads over the River Arga.

The peaceful tracks from Puente la Reina to Estella meanders along rolling farmland,passing small towns and villages nestled among olive groves,cereal crops and vineyards to a hilltop village (Zirauki) of medieval streets and the best of preserved sketches of Roman road.

The Camino continues to the monuments of Estella and the free wine fountain at the museum of Bodegas Irache. Most of the walk tracks among vineyards,olive trees and cereal crops to Los Arcos,where the Camino changes to rolling countryside,where the pilgrim leaves the Navarra and enters the La Rioja region,famous for its red wines.Passing from the dramatic ruins of Clavijo castle to the regions capital city of Largona is capped with the best of Tapas and Rioja-style food specialties.

" Faith is the bird that feels the height
and sings while the dawns still dark."

-Lagore.

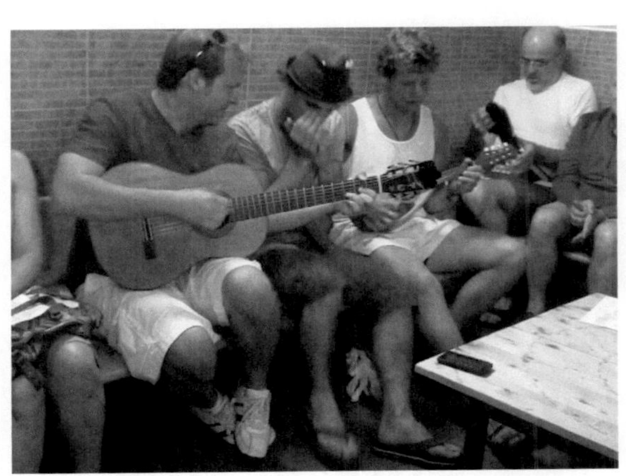

CAMINOWAY.COM.AU
"A journey of the Spirit"

Section 2 DARKNESS TO LIGHT

If music be the food of love play on.
Give me excess of it,that surfeiting,
the appetite may sicken,and so die.

Twelfth Night Act 1,scene 1,1-3

-William Shakespeare.

My journey to the muses of music may not have happened,if it was not for the chance meeting of a young German musician,Robin Marien of the then group "Uritup".We had been walking together for a couple of days discussing life and music.Our little band of brothers included his mate Roland,Dan from the Czech Republic,Young,a Korean born New Yorker and myself.Robin and Roland worked together supporting refugees as their nine to five jobs and Robin moonlighted at night with rock n' roll concerts and weekend gigs.The group was in production of their third album at the time of our chance meeting. The second album "Overcome" was making some headway in the chart as was their concerts.However,I could sense a change in Robin growing approach to his musical direction,as we walked along together.We both agreed not to give up our day job and a sentence from the Desiderata came to mind as we walked "Enjoy your achievement as well as your plans.Keep interested in your own career however humble,it is a real possession in the changing fortunes of time."

Roland was our catalyst on the journey as you may have well read in my novel "The Sword of Discernment", but suffice to say here,that he fell behind us and we left him many motivational signs along the Way to help him keep his spirits up.The sign writing was a distraction from the weight of our heavy pack and ever present blistered feet and the extreme heat of the Spanish summer.Dan was like a guardian angel with his dry sense of humour and ability to live on coca cola.Young was a guiding light to me as he shared the dark side of his life and I likewise did with him.They had become for me,over the course of days we walked together ,my little band of brothers,and a soothing stepping stone in nurturing my inner child.We stayed at many Pilgrim hostels together on our journey towards Santiago.Robin often entertained us,whenever he got his hands on a guitar.It seemed like a guitar would always turn up when Robin was around.One night at a hostel,he turned from his usual heavy rock to singing a beautiful ballad called "The Mountain side". He had written it after listening to a childhood story of one of his client refugees back in Germany.I suggested he might consider folk music as an alternative to his heavy metal rock,as he was really good at singing ballads.It proved after his Camino, to be the direction he has taken, as the taste for music with the young in Europe has returned to folk.By way of example of a country folk idea,I recited to Robin a song I had written, on the train trip from Paris to St-Jean-Pied-de-Port,about my Grandfather entitled "The Boundary Rider."

When I returned to Australia after the Camino,I received an email from Robin asking me for the lyrics to 'The Boundary Rider' as he wanted to write his own chord music to the song. Being limited to lyrics and melody,I was happy to oblige,except that I had not written a chorus yet,so I sent him some lyrics for a song about my drinking days with my Father instead and promised to send him the finished production of the Boundary Rider once I had written a chorus.He wrote back that he liked the lyrics a lot and said it turned him to tears when he read it.Meanwhile,his interest in my songs sparked a surge of creativity in me and I wrote a chorus for the Boundary Rider and sent him the complete lyrics. As a result of my chance meeting with Robin,I am in currently in the production faze of an album of my songs,have completed a novel of my Camino adventure and this book of prose. Every persons life is a Camino and in my case,a new direction.It is my firm belief that the song writing and stories I tell would not have happened had I not ventured to the Way.

Boundary Rider

Well I've been a boundary rider,
on the wild New England range,
rounded up range cattle,
driven more across the plains.

Oh! I learned to live the bush way
when I was just a kid,
camping out with my ole granddad,
cutting timbers what he did.

I've had my share of hard times,
I've had my fill of pain,
if I had my time back over,
probably do it all again.

Killing dingoes when in danger,
cooking rabbit to survive,
staying warm at nights log fire,
sleeping out when I was five.

Well I crossed the barren desert,
and I tramped the hills alone,
made it through some swollen rivers,
wild dust storms and chilly snows.

Cause I've been an over lander,
it was the life I 'd lived,
If I had my time back over,
probably do it all again.

" Hear the thunder on the mountain,
It's the brumbies on the run,
see the murder of the black crows,
as they greet the morning sun."

"Feel the gentle chill of first light.
tea and damper's almost done,
breaking camp we long to start out,
saddle up for boundary run."

Well my granddad was a drover,
cross the country he did roam,
seeking out his heart's companion,
where he found his heart and home.

Boxed in tents for Jimmy Sharman,
tried to earn a decent quid,
carried swag across the Darling,
seeking work that's what he did.

He cut timber on the north coast,
drove cattle on the plain,
shore sheep west of Tamworth,
in those good old country days.

Panned for gold in old Kalgoorlie,
strut the boards and sang on stage,
did his share of hard core drinking,
in the good old country ways.

Once he sat on his verandah,
telling stories to grandkids,
of the life he'd left behind him,
and the things that he once did.

So I sing this song for granddad,
in my heart he will remain,
cause he was a boundary rider,
on the wild New England range.

"Hear the thunder on the mountain,
it's the brumbies on the run,
see the murder of the black crows,
as they greet the morning sun."

"Feel the gentle chill of first light,
tea and dampers almost done,
breaking camp we long to start out,
saddle up for boundary run".

"He was my hero but he died and I let go and now I let God."

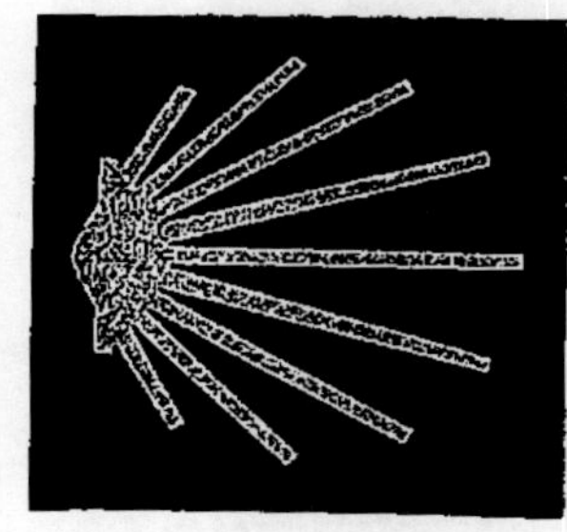

Dad and days Gone.

I saw you stumble,
I felt your fall,
from some great height,
on your ....majestic wall.

The mind's eyes weeping,
what a ghostly tale,
as you went struggling
................down that trail.

Well I watched you rise,
to a world of fame,
in some midnight madness,
on a lonely plain.

Like you the light blazed,
a bright road for me,
It only lead too,
lead too................misery.

Thou you could not see,
the rot set in,
t'was when I followed,
drinking drink again.

I followed your footsteps,
down the dark lit path,
on my way out,
it could not last .

"You were my hero
dear love,good old dad,
a drinking companion
some good times we had
but mostly just sadness,
for the things left undone.

No more cymbals nor chimes,
no more beat of the drum."

Like you in the power,
once bitten by wine,
gripped by the grape,
stumbling blind,
I found my way out,
through a tormented mind,
a power that answers,
much greater than mine.

So where is the oil rag?
where is the grime?
lost in the rhythm,
that rambles to rhyme,
passed by the footsteps,
in shades of time,
the engineer drowned,
..........in a fog of wine.

Well I watched you rise,
to a world of fame,
in some midnight madness,
on a lonely plain.

and I am here now,
biding my time.
Yes.I am here now
biding my time.

" You were my hero,
dear love,good old dad,
a drinking companion,
some good times we had,
but mostly just sadness,
for the things left undone.

No more cymbals nor chimes,
no more beat of the drum."

No more beat of the drum.

No more cymbals nor chimes,
no more beat of the drum.

No more beat of the drum.

Crowded city blues

Well it's 5 o'clock,
everybody's going home,
to the fridge,the stove,the toaster,
lovers on the phone.

Well I walk along weary,
I've no place to go,
got no money,
guess I'll have to borrow,
I've got the blues,
the crowded city blues.

Well my woman she done left me,
for another man,
took the goods and shackles,
and the kids in hand.

Well I walk along weary,
I've no place to go,
got no money,
guess I'll have to borrow,
I've got the blues,
got the crowded city blues.

Well I got me a job,
got a new woman,
making a living,
no longer in a jam.

No more walk along weary,
got me places to go,
got me some money,
don't need to borrow,
no more the blues.
no more the crowded city blues.

Well my woman's a singer,
in a rhythm band,
she's a groove mother,
we work hand in hand,

Never world weary,
we've got places to go,
making a living,
just putting on a show.
we call the blues,
we call ,
the crowded city blues!

Well it's 5 o'clock,
everybody's going home,
to the fridge ,the stove,the toaster,
lovers on the phone.

Well my woman she done left me,
for another man,
took the goods and shackles,
and the kids in hand.

Well I got me a job,
got a new woman,
making a living,
no longer in a jam.

Well my woman's a singer,
in a rhythm band,
she's a groove mother,
we work hand in hand.

Never world weary,
we've got places to go,
making a living,
just put on a show,
we call the blues,
we call,
the crowded city blues!

Longing for Baby

There's a tear in my eye,
as I strum my guitar,
looking out on the ocean blue,
seeing you in a dream,
as the pale moon beams,
hunting my love in a tune.

Yes I am leaving today,
for a world far away,
singing this song of hope,
seeing you in my arms,
loving you in my care.

Oh! Baby I'm longing for you!
Yeah,Baby I'm longing for you.

Oh! I am my own tune maker,
in a voice of vision it seems,
hanging to a melody ,
awake to my guttered dreams.

There's a rhythm in my magic,
for I pluck the chords so fair,
with visions of your ruby lips,
majestic colours in your hair.

Oh! baby I'm longing for you.
Yeah baby I'm longing for you.

Yes I'm calling this love,
floating over the blue,
watching the rainbows end,
moves to my beat,
in the depth of the shrew.

Oh!baby I'm longing for you.
Yeah!baby I'm longing for you.

I am my own tune maker,
in a voice of vision it seems,
hanging on to a melody,
awake to my guttered dreams.

There's rhythm in my magic,
for I pluck the chord so fair,
with vision of your ruby lips,
majestic colours in your hair.

Oh! Baby I'm longing for you,
Baby I'm longing for you.

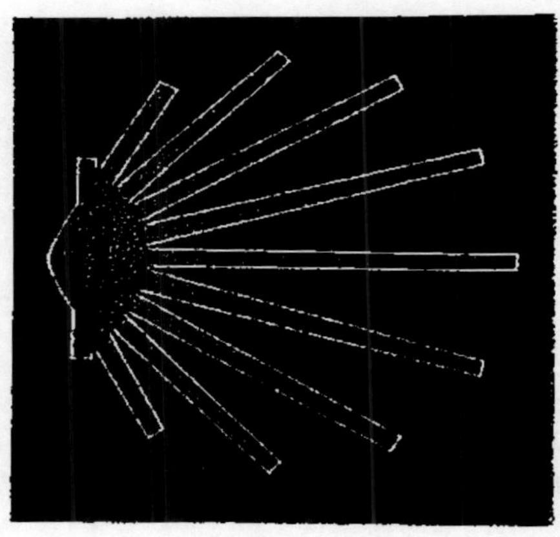

"The drum beat of the heart of my Camino is in tune with the rhythm of my feet."

The loner (James Dean).

When I was a young man,
I watched the movie screen,
my hero was a loner,
by the name of James Dean.

Now Jimmy was a wild one,
gave his heart to every role,
he had trained in method acting,
he acted with his soul.

James Dean,James Dean,
larger than life on the silver screen.

It is said the good die first,
whilst the living just get old,
and their hearts just get harder,
and their living is controlled.

It was not that way for jimmy,
he was a candle in the wind,
he burnt it in the middle,
and he lit it at both ends.

James Dean,James Dean,
larger than life on the silver screen.

James Dean,James Dean,
larger than life on the silver screen.

Well he only made three movies,
masterpieces because of him,
he was a wild rebellious youth,
and I admired him,

In the movie " East of Eden",
his soul search was the plot,
for we saw a son rejected,
by a mother who was lost.

In "Giant" he was an outsider,
hated by self made men,
then he struck it rich with oil,
and he stuck it up to them.

The climax of his acting,
T'was "rebel without a cause"
played himself with all his heart,
but it killed him in the end.

James Dean,James Dean,
larger than life on the silver screen.

James Dean,James Dean,
larger than life on the silver screen

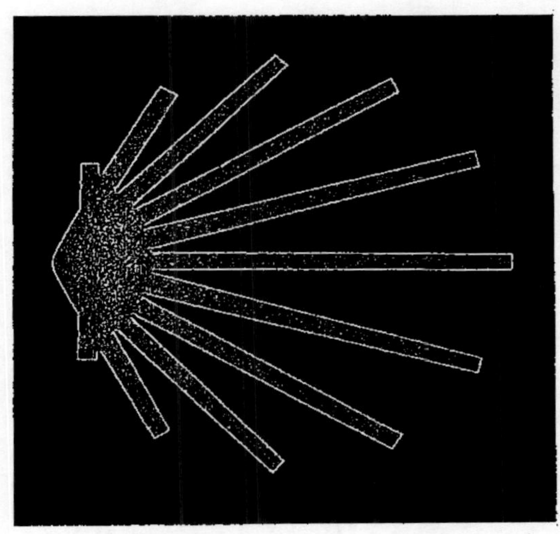

"You've got to know when love is over,
You've got to learn to carry on,
and with the world upon your shoulder,
you find a way to carry on....."

- Michael Bolton Lyrics.

Wounded love heart.

Now my heart beats
to a drummer,
not quite the same as the rest,
where I long to be free ,
attuned with the sound in my chest.

Listen to the rhythm of a heart beat,
the sound of a different drum,
not the beat of a heart for another,
nor the weary heart wounded by love.

It won't be found in worldly values,
where money's the ultimate quest,
not the beat of a heart in battle,
where they pin a medal
on your breast.

It may be found when in tune with nature,
where man is at one with the plan,
climbing a rugged mountain range,
tilling and planting the land.

Sailing the blue of the ocean,
viewing the flight of a bird,
hearing the sound of cicada,
deep in a forested wood.

Catching a fish for survival,
cooking it on one's own fire,
sleeping out in the open,
watching the star filled sky.

Seeing the sunrise at dawning,
plainly being in tune,
living the now when it's crowded,
being quite still in a room.

It's being in tune with ones senses,
the music you have in your heart,
conscious of each passing moment,
the wounded love heart's where you start.

It won't be found in worldly values,
where monies the ultimate quest,
not the beat of a heart in battle,
Where they pin a medal
on your breast.

Now I know my heart beats
to a drummer.
that's not quite the same as the rest,
It's where I long to be free,
attuned with the sound in my chest.

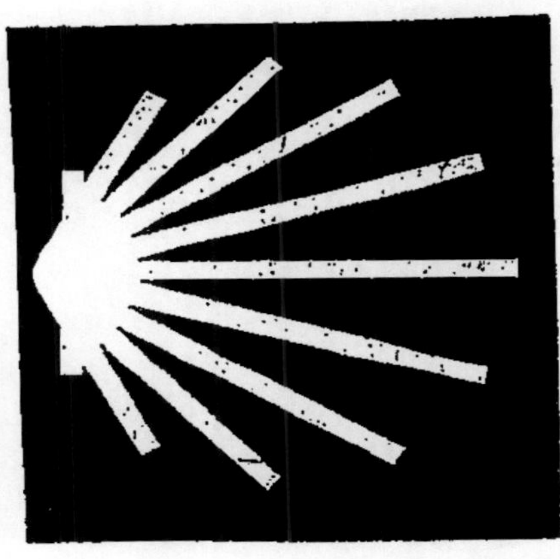

"...without a flaw in the character of my darkness I would not shed light."

Phil Ochs folk singer(song version)

There was once a poor boy,
from old El Paso town,
loved his life and family,
father came back from war,
a torn and shattered man,
mother turned her back on them.

He graduated military school,
gave up university,
took off to New York City,
the goal was political left,
civil rights was his cause,
Phil Ochs was here & there for peace.

Well he worked the streets alone,
singing protest songs he wrote,
on the latest news and current events,
in the streets of Greenwich village,
he organised protest rallies,
Phil Ochs was there to stop a war.

"Once there was a folk singer,
who busked out on the street,
he sang out with a cause,
for peace,
a voice without fame,
stood ragged in the rain,
seemed to him his cause was lost.'

He sang the cause of Luther King,
did The same for JFK,
saw him as the father of the nation,
but the bullets came so fast,
and in their dying gasp,
the words of peace their epitaph.

Phil renewed his fate filled plea,
worked for Bob Kennedy,
the one last hope for liberty,
but the night the shots rang out,
folk singer died some that day,
another hero laying in his grave.

Phil Ochs left the village scene,
no way out for him it seemed,
he travelled the world so lost,
looked for another cause,
recorded for no applause,
time was running out for him.

"Once there was a folk singer,
who busked out on the street,
he sang out with a cause,
for peace,
a voice without fame,
stood ragged in the rain,
seemed to him his cause was lost."

Phil tuned up his guitar,
when he met Victor Jara,
the heroic Chile folk singer,
they sang of need for change,
life was being rearranged,
life was coming to its end for them.

Oh!the moon it turned blood red,
when Salvadore's Chile fell,
a victim of a coup d'etat!
it was on that fate filled night,
Victor Jara lost his life,
Chile's voice of peace was dead.

Phil Ochs rose to the cause,
a concert to end wars,
the benefit for Jara's family,
so he sang his final song,
and he left this mortal coil,
a sad theme was his last song.

"Once there was a folk singer,
who busked out on the street,
he sang out with a cause,
for peace,
a voice without fame,
stood ragged in the rain,
seemed to him his cause was lost"

O'Gormans' by the fire.

When the sun shines on the mountain,
you can see a little town,
were the children play in dream time,
were happiness seems to be born.

Scattered memories in the dreaming,
visions of some distant scene,
return to me now in the midnight hour,
shades of smoke in this misty dream.

Loving memories of fun and laughter,
flash across the flaming night,
forging family life time bonds,
whilst the children sing their tunes.

Run inside,
sit with your dreams by the fire side,
run inside,
new dreams can still be born.

In those days of wine and roses,
were friendships once were bound,
scattered memories fill the mind now,
by the hearth and flaming fire!

Oh!the night was turning black ,
as the flames grew higher and higher,
and the embers turn to golden stars,
at O'Gormans by the fire!

Yeah,we had so many good times,
great friendships way back when,
singing children and stories telling,
at O'Gormans by the fire.!

Run inside,
sit with your dreams by the fire side,
run inside,
new dreams can still be born.

Oh!The flames were rising higher,
when the night was closing in,
we drank wine with whiskey chasers,
and we stayed warm by the fire.

When the sun shines on the mountain,
You can see a little town,
smoke rising from the chimneys,
where the fire side heaths die down.

People out there in the village morn,
on their way to daily chores,
facing bitter cold and sleet now,
dressed up to keep them warm.

Run inside,
sit with your dreams by the fire side,
run inside,
new dreams can still be born.

Mist is rising from a dark night,
all is quiet and the air is clean,
in the little village hamlet,
where once I lived out my dreams.

Oh! I awake now stretch and yawning,
from the wonder of my dream,
shattered memories and desolation,
of a life that's forever gone.

Run inside,
sit with your dreams by the fire side,
run inside,
new dreams can still be born.

Oh! The days of wine and roses,
and our life in fields of dreams,
distant recall of golden friendships,
fading memories of fireside scenes.

We had so many good times,
questioning life and what it means,
times of rounding,roping and riding,
in our worn out boots and jeans.

Oh! I take to the road singing,
plucking on my old banjo,
singing this song of distant memories,
of loves now lost in dreams.

Run inside,
sit with your dreams by the fire side,
run inside,
new dreams can still be born.

Run inside,
sit with your dreams by the fire side,
run inside,
new dreams can still be born.

On the road to Santiago.

There's a story that the Christ man told,
of a pilgrim on his way,
from Jerusalem to Jericho,
on that fate filled day.

Fortune wasn't smiling,
when he came upon some thieves,
they robbed him and they stabbed him,
left him there to bleed.

Now it happen that upon that road,
a priest was passing near,
he saw the young man lying there,
but he passed him by.

Then came a lawyer of business mind,
who had more than he could spend,
he likewise ignored the man,
and on the road he went.

Then came a man both strong and kind,
who put him on his back,
carried him to a near by inn,
just a little way down the track.

He shared with him some of his food,
left money for his keep,
and told the hotel owner,
get him well,I'll pay upkeep.

The man we call a Samaritan,
It's the name of those of kind,
who put others before themselves,
help the poor,the drunk ,the blind.

Now youth today walk on the way
to discover their own soul,
whilst those of us towards our end,
we're letting go our load.

Suffice to say along the way,
the poor and lame just beg,
whilst pilgrims on the Camino,
see naught but what's ahead.

Santiago Travellers,
travelling the Camino way,
doing their own thing,
determined to be free.

Suffice to say along the way,
the poor and lame just beg,
whilst pilgrims on the Camino,
see naught but whats ahead.

Santiago travellers,
doing their own thing,
walking the Camino way,
for the freedom it will bring.

"There's a man walking the Camino way,
he claims no worldly goods,
lives on love for his fellow man,
carries his own cross.

By day and night he helps the poor,
the lame,the blind, the lot.
yes,he is a Samaritan,
on the Camino way!"

"The poor are slowly starving.
as they hold out their beggar tin,
and the unemployed cry out for help,
to find a job for them."

The journey of the Camino ends,
in the church at Santiago,
were pilgrims flock in thousands,
in their final letting go.

The bishop in his mitre,
praised pilgrims with a prayer,
preaching of the dark side gone,
now that we are free to care.

Outside of the cathedral,
the beggars line the doors,
pleading for some help,
from within the sacred walls,

The symbol of the Camino,
is but a scollop shell,
It's many road maps on its back,
has many tales to tell.

Oh! when you turn it over,
It turns into a hand,
the one that remains open,
for our fellow man.

Santiago Travellers,
doing their own thing,
walking the Camino,
determined to be free.

The swagman.

Give me the life I love,
let the old ways wash by me,
keep me cool by an old gum tree,
or a fireside hearth to warm me.

Let me bed down in cave or tent,
by a riverside to bathe me,
such is the life for a man like me,
hot damper and tea to hale me!

Here's the heart to start anew,
whilst the summer lingers,
warmed by autumn's leafy fall,
steeled by winter's bitter.

Give me the life I love,
and the wealth before me,
wealth I have within my heart
hope my soul companion.

So let the burdens fall
were they may,
let what will be wash by me,
give me a blue sky above,
and a bush track before me.

Loves may come and loves may go,
friends are my true reason,
for I seek the track ahead,
with the Southern Cross behind me.

Give me the life I love,
let the old ways wash by me,
keep me cool by an old gum tree,
or a fireside hearth to warm me.

Let me bed down in cave or tent,
by a riverside to bathe me,
such is the life for a man like me,
hot damper and tea to hale me.

So let the seasons come and go,
wherever I may wander,
warmed by love of friends anew,
with no malice to the foe,
nor to life my reason.

Blind me not to springtime swell,
nor yield to come by chance,
not the power of the chase,
just living the bush mans' dance!

So let the burdens fall where they may,
let what will be wash by me,
give me a blue sky above,
and a bush track before me.

Wealth I seek not,love nor hate,
nor a star to guide me,
just the bush track ahead,
with the southern cross behind me.

A Dylan tribute dream.

Yep! Heard an old whistle sounding,
in the midnight of my mind,
saw Bob Dylan riding a boxcar,
reliving Woody Guthrie's dream.

He was singing songs of sadness,
remembering old friends,
of the good times and the hard ones,
when Woody rode freight trains.

It was Dylan's train to glory,
on his everlasting gig,
holding on to his mortality,
remembering how he lived.

Well I saw the pale moon rising,
saw the light upon his face,
and his dream was in my dream,
it was for the human race.

"Oh! I saw his shooting star tonight,
watched it fade away and die,
it was in the midnight of my dream,
Bob Dylan's voice just died."

Oh!the train stopped at the station,
in the cross roads of my mind,
it was then Bob Dylan alighted,
and turned his head to mine.

Yeah!He wore a black cowboy hat
with a red leather band,
and he wore a blue denim shirt
tied with a Wyatt Earp leather string.

He was dressed in black leather jeans,
wore Spanish leather boots,
and he looked so pale and thin,
then his blue eyes burnt sad tunes!

He greeted me with a grin,
and he just walked right in,
he put his guitar down by the door,
and I split a beer with him.

"Oh! I saw his shooting star tonight,
watched it fade away and die,
it was in the middle of my dream,
Bob Dylan's voice just died"

Dylan took over my place,
so I just hung about,
watched him prepare a poster,
for the epitaph of his sound.

It was a promo of his life,
with music and guitar,
in a coat of many colours,
the lyrical folk star.

and many from the other side,
began to gather round,
the man in black came in first,
and Dylan just shook his hand.

Oh!the grand ole Opry singers,
all gathered in my room,
Hank Williams drank with Jimmy Reeves,
Chad Atkins sang an old tune.

"Oh!I saw his shooting star tonight,
watched it fade away and die,
it was in the middle of my dream,
Bob Dylan's voice just died."

In wandered Buddy Holly,
Ritchie Valence and Big Bopper,
their guitars began to play,
sang Peggy Sue for their supper!

And over in a corner,
Woody Guthrie stood alone,
strumming quietly on his guitar,
singing of some old Kentucky home!

Charlie Daniels and Tammy Wynette,
Charlie Pride and Patsy Cline,
Phil Everly and Tom T Hall,
waiting to pick Bob Dylan's mind,

Standing by a protest poster
beside a graffitied wall,
Phil Ochs stood there singing,
a song about James Dean.

"Oh! I saw his shooting star tonight,
watched it fade away and die,
it was in the middle of my dream,
Bob Dylan's voice just died."

Oh!the Kennedy's were looking,
at a photo of Che Guevara,
Martin Luther King just shook his head,
Medgar Evers stood crying, admired the red star!

Oh! The room was getting crowded,
with singers of my youth,
and the crowd went very silent,
as Elvis sang a song.

Pete Seeger strummed an old banjo,
singing his Kumbaya
Paddy and Tom Clancy joined in,
Tommy Makem singing from afar!

and I saw Jimmy Morrison,
Janis Joplin and Keith Moon,
Jimmy Hendrix played his guitar,
John Lennon sang a peace tune!

Oh! there were so many faces,
to many it's plain to tell,
all gathered just for Dylan,
to give tribute and farewell.

"Well I saw his shooting star tonight,
watched it fade away and die,
it was in the midnight of my dream,
Bob Dylan's voice just died."

Yeah! He wore a black cowboy hat,
with a red leather band,
and he wore a blue denim shirt,
tied with a Wyatt Earp string.

He was dressed in black leather jeans,
wore Spanish leather boots,
and he looked sp pale and thin,
then his blue eyes burnt sad tunes!

When I awoke this morning,
I copied down this dream,
read the news today oh! boy,
Bob Dylan's still alive!

Section 3-LEAD KINDLY LIGHT

"the longest journey
is the journey inwards.
Of him who has chosen his destiny,
Who has started upon his quest,
For the source of his being." page 58

"The present moment is significant,
not as the bridge between past and future,
but by reason of its contents,
contents which can fill our emptiness
and become ours,if we are capable
of receiving them." page 62

-Dag Hammarskjold, Markings

We are all on a journey inward ,whether or not we are aware of it,embrace it or ignore it,eventually it comes to us.Our final journey is of course death and whatever our skills,efforts and aspirations or the way we meet our inner dragon,death is the only absolute constant.Our Camino of life brings us face to face with many people who are reflections of our own character in our moments of being in their presence.We experience their strength in our weakness and vice versa.

Equally we may be clever or ignorant,rich or poor,good or evil,but eventually we all bow to the great leveller.It has been the belief of human beings throughout the ages that, something survives beyond our physical shell when we get to the other side
Our myths and legends are expressed in imaginative forms of fear,fantasy and expectations.Religion offers certainty about our afterlife,teaching dogmas during our lifetime that guarantee favourable conditions after death if we live a good life.Myths present us with alternatives,metaphors and images which guarantee us nothing,but somehow communicate a meaning and value to death which renders it part of life and a necessary chapter in the great cosmic cycle.

My contemplation on my Camino caused me to look back,reflect,look inward,reflect and face the reality of each day on my journey of the Camino de Santiago and ultimately write down here my poetic imagery of a journey through a living darkness to a new found light.

Section 3-Logrono to Burgos

Leaving Logrono by the old pilgrim's gate ' Puerta del Camino' it is back to the vineyards of La Rioja and on to the 12th Century town of Navarrete built by the "Knights of the Sepulchre" and a pause in the medieval town of Najera and its panoramic views of the whole region.

This is followed by quiet country roads with the La Demanda Mountains to the south.Through the small village of La Rioja dedicated to the region's patron,La Virgen de Valvanera and on to the starting point of the "monasteries route' of the Yuso and Suso monasteries of San Millan de la Cogolla,considered to be the birthplace of the spanish language. Then on to the beautiful city of Santo Domingo,with its close history to Camino de Santiago.

The trail from San Domingo starts on uneven terrain through woodlands and crop field.Near Belorando the Oca Mountains is the last range to be seen before entry into the Meseta,the central Spanish Plateau.The trail takes the pilgrim through pleasant villages and along earthen tracks and nature trails to the peaceful hamlet of San Juan de Ortega.As the pilgrim reaches the mountains of ' Villafranca Montes de Oca',the camino weaves through gorgeous woodlands of oak and pine before reaching San Juan de Ortega.

The way continues across the mountainous terrain of the Sierra de Atapuerca with views of the Burgos region, as the pilgrim descends to reach the river flat valley to the suburbs of Burgos,the home to Spains most beautiful cathedral and the history of El Cid.

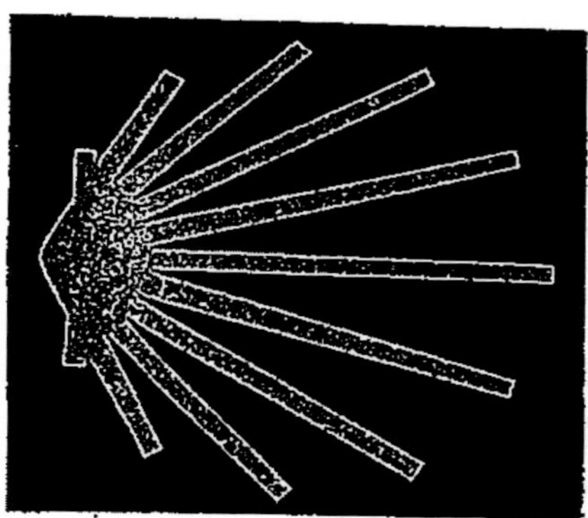

"Seeds of discouragement will not grow in a thankful heart"

-Anonymous.

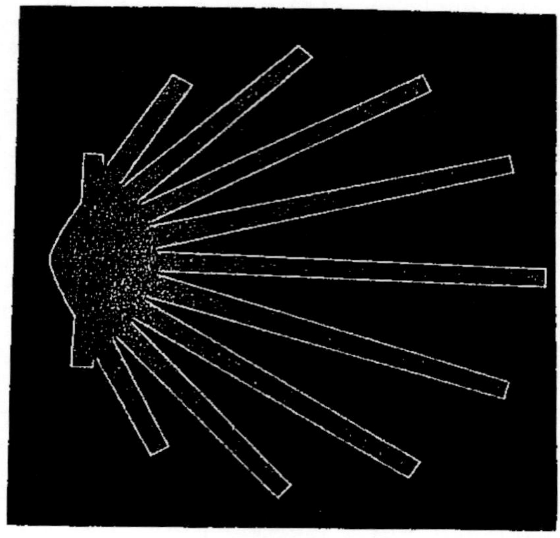

" Hold fast to dreams
for if dreams die,
life is a broken winged bird
that cannot fly.

Hold fast to dreams
for when dreams die,
life is a barren field,
frozen with snow."

-Langston Hughes.

SECTION 3-LEAD KINDLY LIGHT

"Pay attention to the doors that are opening and closing,
and go through the doors that are opened to you."

- Crystal

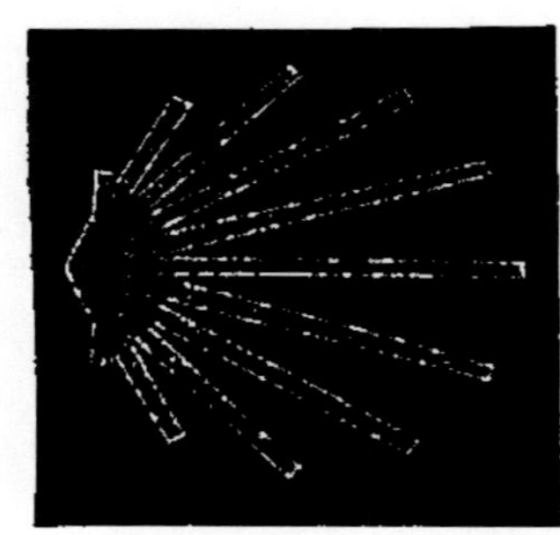

Darkness to Light.

Here I'm walking in my solitude,
in a vast and peaceful place,
meditating on my inner self,
a prince of darkness inhabits this space.

Oh! The masters sitting at a table,
with a white light by his side,
there are three men with green lanterns,
and some angels as his guides.

There are candidates in the darkness,
like ghosts upon the meadow,
their voices pledge eternal vigilance,
as I peer into the shadow.

Oh! I walk through fields of clover,
my eyes on the sky above,
with a flaming star to guide me,
on a mountain path to love.

Now I hear the words of silence,
as I gaze more deep inside,
and I drink the wine from a silver cup,
in obedience and communion.

There's an owl sits on my shoulder,
with wisdom and vigilance,
the Master places a helmet on me,
and a laurel of courage,zeal and honesty.

Then the three wise men step up to me ,
with a quiver of arrows for my shoulder,
order me to speak in tongues of fire,
of power and eloquence bolder.

Oh! I walk through fields of clover,
my eyes on the sky above,
with a flaming star to guide me
on a mountain path to love.

They tie me to a large white column,
to check my moral strength,
gave me a spear of steadfast resolution,
and an implacable shield of clear conscience.

Then I was given a fiery sword,
to fight ridicule and slander,
was my way to be with the prince of peace,
or Lucifer,the architect of plunder.

Oh! My dream took me to Calvary road,
with the prince of dark and light ,
and I realise in my trance filled daze,
both princes died with blood sacrifice.

Oh! I walk through fields of clover,
my eyes on the sky above,
with a flaming star to guide me,
on a mountain path to love.

There were three stones at my feet,
guided by the architect,
saw the great pyramid in wonder,
and stones around my neck!

God gave me cause for justice,
and I kiss my finger tips,
plucked at an old banjo,
put a song upon my lips.

Oh!I came out of the transcending,
on the Camino Way,
lit a white candle in the wind,
hitched my mind's eye to a star.

The God's had for me a vision,
on some future date afar,
so I plucked the chords quite gentle,
to a future folk singing star!

Darkness to light it's the call,
I hear the black crow calling,
Darkness to light it's the call,
I hear the wise old owl.

Oh! I walk through fields of clover,
my eyes on the sky above,
with a flaming star to guide me,
on a mountain path to love.

Fractured heart.

I remember as a little boy,
had a teddy bear,
don't know if it was girl or boy,
just knew it was my friend.

On a dark and cloudy day,
I lost my teddy bear,
it fell into a water grave,
lost forever there.

Something inside me died,
climb down to see my friend,
fell into the darkness,
cried out for the end.

Nobody seemed to know of love.
no one seemed to care,
when you're feeling kind of blue inside,
loves a lost teddy bear.

Fractured heart,fractured heart,
tried so hard to mend this fractured heart,
just got to keep on trying,
before I get to dying,
got to try so hard to mend,
this fractured heart.

There was a girl when as a boy,
she kissed and cuddled me,
one day she just vanished,
she had promised to marry me.

Later on in my teens,
had a girl who was my friend,
we wrote love notes with cupids bow,
But she wounded my heart in the end.

Well loves may come and loves did go,
so many it is plain to see,
kissing and cuddling in the picture show,
making out behind the old oak tree!

Nobody seemed to know of love,
no one seemed to care,
when you're feeling kind of blue inside,
loves a broken hearted fear.

Fractured heart,fractured heart,
tried so hard to mend this fractured heart,
just got to keep on trying,
before I get to dying,
got to try so hard to mend,
this fractured heart.

When I reached a knowing age ,
thought I knew the love game,
music,cars and girls in bars ,
it all seemed quite the same.

Met my love in a music show,
she knew a thing or two,
we often made love into the night,
later we sang the blues.

Well I live life out on the road,
were I've learnt a thing or two,
like,be careful who you depend upon,
cause you'll be left to sing the blues.

Nobody seemed to know of love,
No one seemed to care,
when you're feeling kind of blue,
loves a broken hearted fear.

Fractured heart,fractured heart,
tried so hard to mend this fractured heart,
just got to keep on trying,
before I get to dying,
got to try so hard to mend,
this fractured heart.

The Boatman.

There's a boatman rows the river,
across the Ganges deep and wide,
carrying passengers for rupees,
to reach the other side.

The pay is very meagre ,
he rows by day and night,
and the waters can be danger,
it depend upon the tide.

He rows to feed his family,
and he rows to keep his pride,
carrying passengers for rupees,
and he'll do that till he dies!

There's children work the river,
across the Ganges deep and wide,
clearing garbage from the riverbank ,
just to stay alive.

The pay is very meagre,
and they work by day and night,
recycling their life in slimy waters,
to get rupees for a ride.

Now the boatman's coming for me,
to take me for a ride,
to a land of milk and honey,
in a kingdom on the other side.

He's coming for the living,
on the last day that I survive,
so I'm waiting by the river,
and I'm waiting for change of tide,

Oh! Boatman stay away today,
I'd rather stay alive,
pass me over for another day,
take another upon the tide.

The rivers running quickly,
many boatman row with pride,
ferrying passengers by the hundreds,
to get to the other side.

Now I dream of a flowing river,
milk and honey deep and wide,
were a boatman comes to take me,
to a paradise of my desire.

Oh! waiting at the river's edge,
old Buddha takes my hand,
and he leads me beside still waters,
into the promised land.

Jesus standing next to him,
with a rosary by his side,
praying with stigmata wrists,
whilst the throng strike up the band.

Mother Mary is close by,
with a snake under her foot,
smiles gently at this mortal soul,
checks if I am in the book !

So I'm led besides still waters,
beyond a babbling brook,
to meet the Master of the universe,
on a hilltop we overlook.

Now I'm looking over valley floor,
far beyond the mountain peak,
were the river flows like honey,
and past children dressed well and neat,

In the teeming flowing millions,
they are all there like sheep,
there are no tears or hunger,
just playful without a bleep.

The shepherd leads the flock now,
contented with his lot,
in a land of joy and wonder,
with lush grass and no upkeep.

Now the animals graze contented,
the round ups so up beat,
there's no roping,riding ,rounding,
no need count for cattle or sheep.

I'm surrounded by my next of kin,
with friends and lovers too,
in a land of milk and honey,
and children at my feet.

Oh! I awake from dreaming,
by the river Ganges roar,
see the starving teeming millions,
wanting to know their score.

In the book of life there're many,
they will all get to know,
the day the boatman comes for them,
beyond the overflow.

There's a boatmen rows the river,
across the Ganges deep and wide,
carrying passengers for rupees,
to reach the other side.

There's children work the river,
across the Ganges deep and wide,
clearing garbage from the riverbank,
to get rupees for a ride.

Now the boatman's coming for me ,
to take me for a ride,
to a land of milk and honey,
in a kingdom on the other side.

Oh! Boatman stay away today,
I'd rather stay alive,
pass me over for another day,
take another on the tide.

The river Ganges long and deep,
the rivers deep and wide,
and there's teeming starving millions,
wanting to get to the other side.

Oh!boatman pass me over,
pass me over for another day,
I am not ready for milk and honey land,
or the rupees to pay the way,

Oh!boatman pass me over,
pass me over for another day,
another day,
pass me over for another day.

Oh!boatman pass me over,
pass me over for another day,
another day,
pass me over for another day.

I will be happy.This assumes to be true what Abraham Lincoln said "........... that folks are as happy as they make up their mind to be."

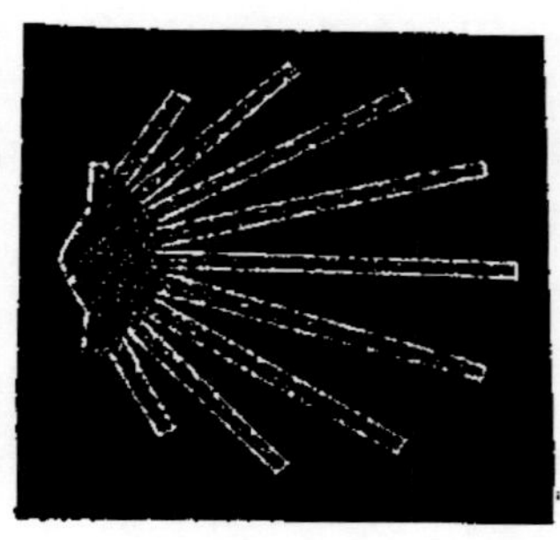

Walking in my shadow.

Do you see a flaming star,
when you walk in clover fields,
is God in your mind's eye,
or in your shadow.

My mind is in a dream,
walking this Camino path,
you are here appearing,
as my shadow.

So you stay close by my side,
as I watched the pale moon rise,
you are here appearing,
as my shadow.

"So I sing out loud and clear,
Love me,love me.
Love me dear,hold on now,
before I am invisible."

Oh! You listen as I sing,
some unfamiliar theme,
you are here appearing
as my shadow.

You are not here or there,
can't touch you with my hand,
cast my trouble to the wind,
and to my shadow,

Now I'm calling no place home,
just walking here alone,
heart set on my flaming star,
you are my shadow.

"So I sing out load and clear,
Love me,love me,
Love me dear,hold on now,
before I am invisible."

Just walking in a dream,
archers arrows point the way,
gold dust walks my feet,
followed by my shadow.

This world's turned dark and grey,
my shadows left me alone,
and God's a stoney path,
yes,he's my shadow.

Yeah! I cry out to the moon,
singing a happy tune,
casting fortune to the wind,
and to my shadow.

"So I sing out load and clear,
Love me,love me,
Love me dear,hold on now
before I am Invisible."

I have the choice to be rich or poor,
take the pleasures as I will,
or just trudge this happy road,
to my destiny.

See my star shines bright,
as I walk into the night,
the moon has clouded now,
and my shadow's gone.

So I have my flaming star,
as I walk the Camino way,
Singing,"love me,love me,
love me,
I am invisible."

Lead kindly light.

Lead kindly light,
lead thou me on,
keep thou my feet,
upon the path I'm on.

Let me not falter,
to climb the highest hill,
view peaceful valleys,
were I'll at last be still.

Foxes have holes,
birds have their nest,
but this son of man,
has no place to rest.

Break me the marble ,
that hardens my heart,
pavements of stone,
were I walk this path.

" Were are you now,
my sweet foreign maid,
here in this light,
that burns in my brain."

This weary pilgrim,
wanders on alone,
broken and shattered,
in search of a home.

Foxes have holes,
birds have their nest,
but this son of man,
has no place to rest.

Foxes have holes,
birds have their nest,
but this son of man,
has no place to rest.

You are my soul companion,
walking the Camino way,
here in my heart,
today and yesterday.

"Were are you now,
my sweet foreign maid,
here in this light,
that burns in my brain."

" Were are you now,
my sweet foreign maid,
fleeting the fire,
that burns in my veins."

Foxes have holes,
birds have their nest,
but this son of man,
has no place to rest.

This son of man,
is longing for breast,
this son of man,
has no place to rest.

" Were are you now,.
my sweet foreign maid,
longing for shelter,
to die in your arms."

Wandering Man

There is a place on the other side,
between two oceans of the great divide,
it's hot by day and cold by night,
no soul water to keep you satisfied.

Now Satan's busy stoking the fire,
his shadow's spitting flames of desire,
ankle deep in the desert sand,
no relief there for a wandering man.

There is a sound on the other side,
between two oceans of the great divide,
were the wind blows eerie carrion calls,
to give up the battle & just end it all.

"Lay down your burden wandering man,
to a place called the promised land,
beside still waters running deep,
milk and honey to quench your peace. "

"Lay down your burden wandering man,
go deep inside to the inner man,
lay down your burden wandering man,
you're on your way to the promised land."

There's a haunting face that's never gone,
were the devil's laughter pours out his scorn,
it's late now for your fate is sealed,
lay down your burden like a fool you'll kneel.

It's growing cold and quiet here still,
as the bleakest crow shrieks a carrion chill,
the dark lit eyes penetrate your heart,
now the old black crows afraid of the dark.

In a desert dream down deep inside,
between two oceans of the great divide,
saw millions living both big and small,
in a place of peace for one and all.

"Lay down your burden wandering man,
to a place called the promised land,
beside still waters running deep,
milk and honey quench your inner peace.

Lay down your burden wandering man,
go deep inside to the inner land,
lay down your burden wandering man,
You're on your way to the promised land."

Yeah! there's a place on the other side,
between two oceans of the great divide,
were palm trees sway in a golden land,
& honey milk waters keep you satisfied.

There is light on the other side,
between two oceans of the great divide,
it's peace by day and calm by night,
were holy waters keep you satisfied.

Satan never sleeps its true to say,
his shadows fading in an endless cue,
ankle deep in a river of blood,
he's drowning now for a wandering man.

"Lay down your burden wandering man,
to a place called the promised land,
beside still waters running deep,
milk and honey to quench your peace."

"Lay down your burden wandering man,
go deep inside to the inner man,
lay down your burden wandering man
you're on your way to the promised land."

Wandering man Oh! Wandering man,
touch the finger of God,
in the promised land,
touch the finger of God,
in the promised land.

"In letting my feet do the walking I can be still,
be still and know that I am God."

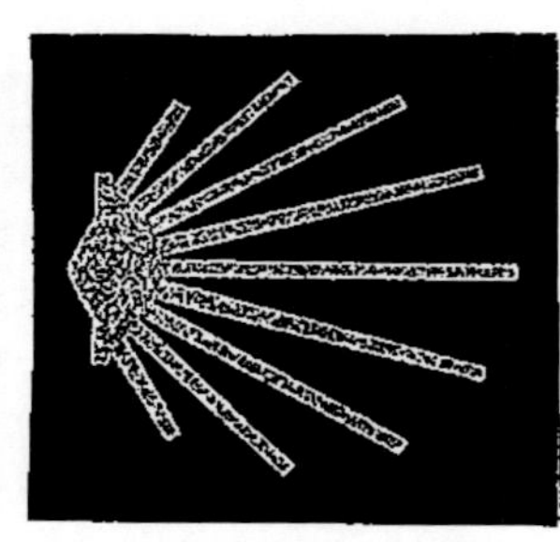

Hurdy-gurdy man.

Riding on the wheel of life,
on the outside looking in,
like a child on a merry go round,
in an ever eternal spin!

Riding on the wheel of life.
on the outside looking in,
like a monkey chained to a hurdy-gurdy
whilst the master churns the thing!

Hurdy-gurdy noise,
hurdy-gurdy noise,
the wheel is still in spin,
listen to the carrion call,
beneath the constant din.

Riding on the wheel of life,
on the inside looking out,
like a rider on the wheel of death,
in a death defying bout!

Riding on the wheel of life,
on the outside looking in,
falling into the dragon's mouth,
were a lotus flower begins!

Hurdy-gurdy noise,
Hurdy-gurdy noise,
the wheel is till in spin,
listen to the carrion call,
beneath the constant din!

Riding on the wheel of life,
on the inside looking out,
loving within the lotus flower,
were love and death do sprout!

Riding on the wheel of life,
on the inside looking out,
embraced in the arms of love,
united in the flower!

Hurdy-gurdy noise,
hurdy-gurdy noise,
the wheel is still in spin,
listen to the carrion call,
beneath the constant din!

Riding on the wheel of life,
on the outside looking in,
casting light into the dark,
we are powerless in the spin!

Hurdy-gurdy noise,
Hurdy-gurdy man,
singing songs of love.

Hurdy-gurdy noise,
hurdy-gurdy man,
singing songs of love.

"I believe in the sun even if it isn't shining,
I believe in love even when I am alone,
I believe in God even when he is silent."

-WW 11 refugee.

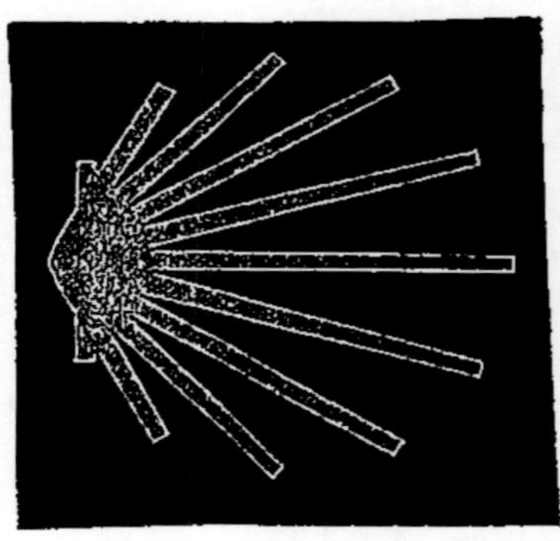

The river and the ocean.

There's a track to mission mountain,
on the pathway of the mind,
in a valley of the spirit,
were flows a gentle stream.

It trickles over cobble stones,
in an ever constant theme,
murmurs a hushed lullaby,
to the birth of its own dream.

Were its silence can be broken,
distracted by morning glow,
as the dark rolls back the curtain,
to reveal a constant flow.

Hear the silence in the deafness,
by the bright of light eternal,
as the night rolls back the curtain,
to the echo of daylight.

It's flowing is gently onward,
through the valley of the wind,
skimming across the ripple flow,
hasten to a world beyond.

In the deep wall of water flowing,
headlong to the valley floor below,
the spirit river meanders on,
in its mystic constant glow.

There's a child upon the waters,
cast out to nature's way,
he trims his sail to glory,
paddling his own canoe.

Now the water flows are plenty,
as the river journeys on,
headlong to the valley floor,
were it's spirit river flows.

The rivers constant journey,
meets the oceans of the blue,
flowing ever onward,
an ever eternal thing!

The oceans source is reckless,
tied to the will of the moon,
in waves of constant motion,
on a hidden dynamic theme.

The oceans rise and swelling,
in a dark mysterious depth,
attuned to an unknown orchestra,
to the power of a conductor's whim!

Within the winds of chance ,
beyond the ocean blue,
the tide is rushing in,
as waves sounding out glory,
an ever constant din!

There is a vision splendid,
beyond the great divide,
in a source of godly purpose,
to the river and ocean wide!

There's a child upon the waters,
cast out to nature's way,
he trims his sail to glory,
paddling his own canoe!

The life reminder (song version)

There is a life reminder,
awaking in my womb,
It is a strange reflection,
within a harvest moon.

There is a soul of black light,
piercing the impenetrable dark,
it is a strange reflection,
the pain within my heart.

Oh!There is a joy of living,
within the darkest hour,
the power of my candle light,
to germinate your flower.

"No It's not there in the morning glow,
nor in the evening light,
It's a view of some strange reflection,
on the other side of midnight!"

Here we are on the other side,
the other side of midnight,
here we are on the other side,
the other side of midnight.

You may have felt this stud,
reflected in a shooting star,
a mirrored midnight madness
where God seems not to care.

Oh! light maybe burning bright tonight
as you view the universe,
and your soul struggles for some peace ,
whilst my heads is full of verse.

Maybe you're seeing fattened calf,
that feeds the chosen few,
or you glimpse the starving millions,
in the eyes of a film crew.

No,it's not there in the morning glow,
nor in the evening light,
It's a view of some strange reflection,
on the other side of midnight.

Here we are on the other side,
the other side of midnight,
here we are on the other side,
the other side of midnight.

Do you see the warring leaders,
the bodies,dead and burnt,
do you hear the learned gentry sing ,
the chant of some beggar's tune.

Do you cry there in the darkest hour,
whilst planes are dropping bombs,
shaking fear in your emotions,
as you die here in my arms.

Is it the fear in the bewitched,
before the morning glow,
do hear the children crying
or is it some old crow ?

No, it's not there in the morning glow,
nor in the evening light,
It's a view of some strange reflection,
on the other side of midnight.

Here we are on the other side,
the other side of midnight,
here we are on the other side,
the other side of midnight.

Is it me you hear in the moaning cry,
maybe it's that old black crow again,
In the darkness of our dawning light,
loves embrace within our glands.

Oh! I know not when I lost the dream,
maybe when my brain did scream,
for a little bit of peace inside,
to let go of this drugged filled scene.

Yeah! I saw the four horsemen riding,
towards the end of the universe,
spreading fire ,disease and pestilence,
to the peoples of the earth.

No it's not there in the morning glow,
nor in the evening light,
It's a view of some strange reflection,
on the other side of midnight,

Here we are on the others side,
the other side of midnight,
here we are on the other side,
the other side of midnight.

It was whilst I was entwined,
in the flesh of my lover's charms,
riding my wild women,
her pale fear in my arms.

Here we are in the growing light,
It's the hour before the dawn,
holding on in our nakedness,
you are so soft and warm.

Now maybe the end is sooner,
than a man can even blink,
It can be very scaring dreaming,
when you first give up the drink.

So I'm calling out to God now,
alone in the dead of night,
afraid to go to sleep,
please don't turn out the light.

It's not there in the morning glow,
nor in the evening light,
it's the view of some strange reflection,
on the other side of midnight.

Here we are on the other side,
the other side of midnight,
here we are on the other side,
the other side of midnight.

"Reflect upon your present blessings,
of which every man has many,
not upon past misfortunes,
of which all men have some."

-Charles Dickens

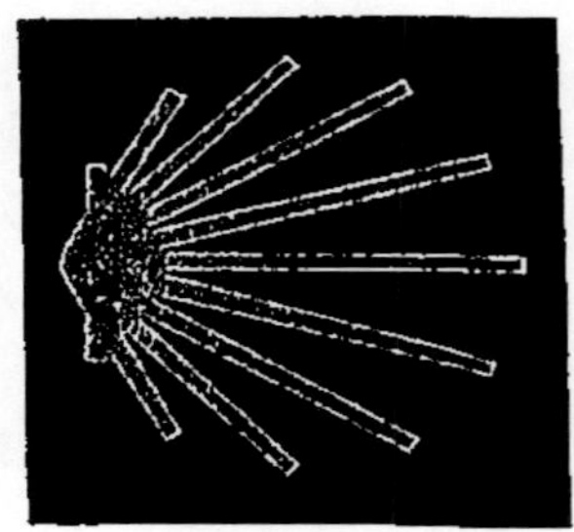

Section 4-Burgos to Sahagun

Leaving the majestic city of Burgos and its medieval grandeur and the promenade on the banks of the Duero and Arlanza rivers the pilgrim enters the Meseta.Walking among immense crop fields across small woods of holm oak and conifers to the medieval stronghold of Hornillos del Camino.Another day of walking in the peaceful vastness of the Meseta,to climb gradually up to the plateau before descending to the valley of the river Bol and the pretty town of Castrojeriz and its 9th century hilltop castle.

A final walk on the plain of the Burgos region to the highest point of the Mesta,Alto Mosterales. After crossing the Pisuera river the way enters the Palencia plans of 'Tierra de Campos',land of the fields and the gothic architecture of its 14th century church.The way , approaching Fromista and the 18th century ,canal de castilla.

The scenic route at Poblacion de Campos follows the peaceful banks of the Ucieza river to Carrion de los Condes.The natural track then follows the old Roman road on its original paved surface which was historically used by French pilgrims on their way to Santiago.

The walk then is full of little valleys which makes the route tougher as it emerges along peaceful; oak woods and cereal fields. Here the pilgrim crosses the river Valderaduey into the province of Leon to the medieval town of Sahagun in the heart of the Meseta.

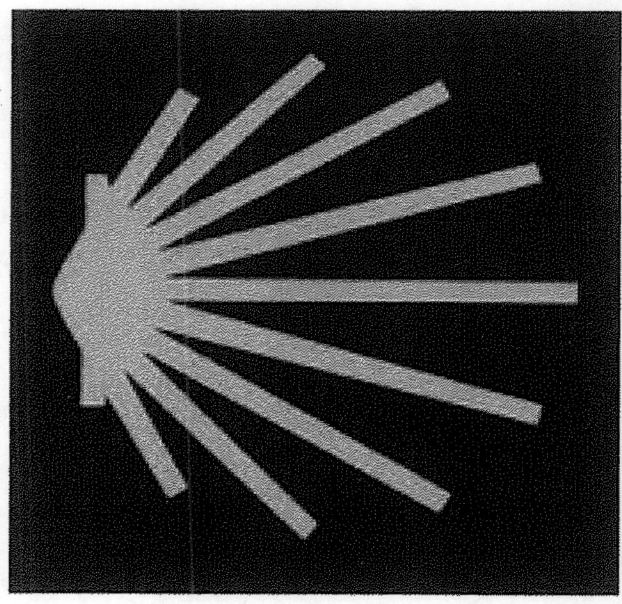

Section 4-Burgos to Sahagun

Leaving the majestic city of Burgos and its medieval grandeur and the promenade on the banks of the Duero and Arlanza rivers the pilgrim enters the Meseta.Walking among immense crop fields across small woods of holm oak and conifers to the medieval stronghold of Hornillos del Camino.Another day of walking in the peaceful vastness of the Meseta,to climb gradually up to the plateau before descending to the valley of the river Bol and the pretty town of Castrojeriz and its 9th century hilltop castle.

A final walk on the plain of the Burgos region to the highest point of the Mesta,Alto Mosterales. After crossing the Pisuera river the way enters the Palencia plans of 'Tierra de Campos',land of the fields and the gothic architecture of its 14th century church.The way , approaching Fromista and the 18th century ,canal de castilla.

The scenic route at Poblacion de Campos follows the peaceful banks of the Ucieza river to Carrion de los Condes.The natural track then follows the old Roman road on its original paved surface which was historically used by French pilgrims on their way to Santiago.

The walk then is full of little valleys which makes the route tougher as it emerges along peaceful; oak woods and cereal fields. Here the pilgrim crosses the river Valderaduey into the province of Leon to the medieval town of Sahagun in the heart of the Meseta.

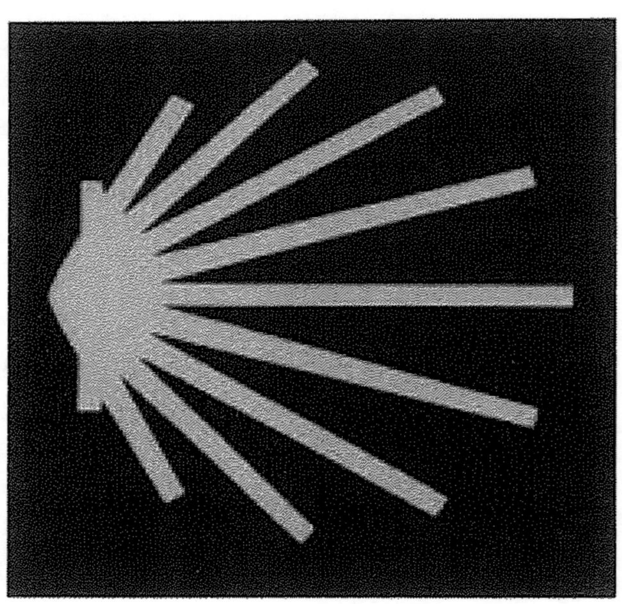

Section 4 SHOOTERS AND DREAMERS

"Go confidently in the direction of your dreams.
Live the life that you imagined."

-Henry David Thoreau

The movie 'Dead Poets Society' has a line "sucking the marrow out of life" . It was the philosopher Henry David Thoreau dictum to live life according to its dictate of simplicity,independence,magnanimity and trust and to live life to the full.Oh! but should disaster strike,one needs to know how to recover from set backs in living such a philosophy in ever day life.I guess we always draw some solace from our heroes when stepping out beyond the normal scope of human experience.

In our youthful quests for meaning ,we seek to define who and what we are, and search for a sense of uniqueness which can reflect a sense of individual purpose and destiny.The meaning for youth is often encountered on life experiences rather than the goal of conscious quest.Later in life, we are more aware of the greater whole of which we are a part and the continuity of generations in which we partake only for a short span.Meaning for the old,may lie involuntarily exploring life's deeper mysteries and a sense of unity which generate compassion,detachment and awareness of spiritual realities.Meaning is usually expressed as a conscious goal when the attraction of the outer world has faded.Conversely,meaning for youth is often a highly egocentric pursuit,just as it should be,a vague beckoning light which gives magic passion,impetus and direction.

We each call for heroes whom we admire and can emulate,who gives us confidence in our choice of direction in living the dream.Our heroes are the symbols of our myth and ideals that largely define us and the limits of our aspirations.We all have some form of hero worship.It never hurts to remind ourselves who our heroes are and for that matter,who they were and what we have learnt from the experience of hero worship,what we are becoming and who indeed are our heroes now.

The Camino had me reflect on many things,not the least of which was heroes and villains,and those whose stories reflected a life that has passed.The reality of the fact that I had no need for heroes which put me in the category of the old.The lessons of the Camino was telling me to live,really live and not to concern my self with heroes but it is good to reflect.Reflect on what heroes meant for me,reflect on my destiny,reflect on the changing world,those who have had a bigger agenda than the masses of man are not quite aware or do not want to know about.Reflect on those close to me,both living and dead,who are or have had an influence on my life.

Section 4-Burgos to Sahagun

Leaving the majestic city of Burgos and its medieval grandeur and the promenade on the banks of the Duero and Arlanza rivers the pilgrim enters the Meseta.Walking among immense crop fields across small woods of holm oak and conifers to the medieval stronghold of Hornillos del Camino.Another day of walking in the peaceful vastness of the Meseta,to climb gradually up to the plateau before descending to the valley of the river Bol and the pretty town of Castrojeriz and its 9th century hilltop castle.

A final walk on the plain of the Burgos region to the highest point of the Mesta,Alto Mosterales. After crossing the Pisuera river the way enters the Palencia plans of 'Tierra de Campos',land of the fields and the gothic architecture of its 14th century church.The way , approaching Fromista and the 18th century ,canal de castilla.

The scenic route at Poblacion de Campos follows the peaceful banks of the Ucieza river to Carrion de los Condes.The natural track then follows the old Roman road on its original paved surface which was historically used by French pilgrims on their way to Santiago.

The walk then is full of little valleys which makes the route tougher as it emerges along peaceful; oak woods and cereal fields. Here the pilgrim crosses the river Valderaduey into the province of Leon to the medieval town of Sahagun in the heart of the Meseta.

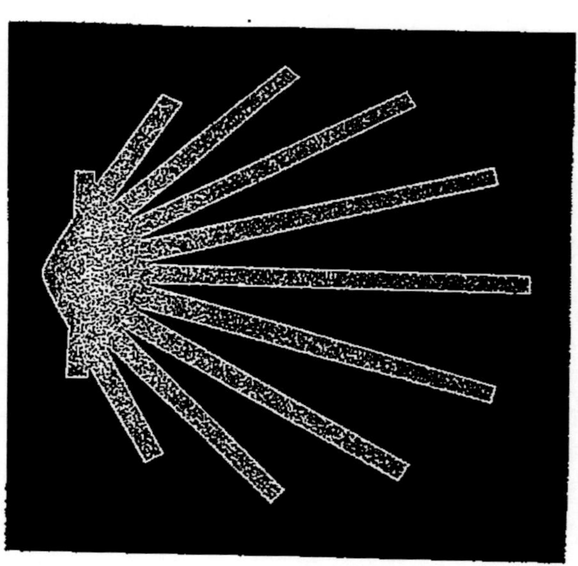

SECTION. 4 SHOOTERS AND DREAMERS

A voice in the wilderness :

Who am "I"? I am "Who am".

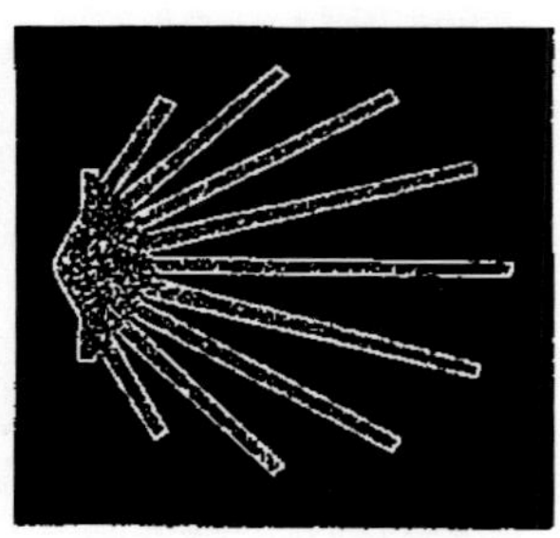

Bobbie Beer,Mountaineer.

This is the story of a wild mountaineer,
goes by the name of Bobbie Beer,
he never walked a mountain track,
never jogged a valley floor,
he just ran up and down them,
cause he ran like Clancy rode them.

Oh! I've walked with Larry the vet,
on many a mountain climb,
strode out with barefoot Bob,
he died but was a friend of mine.

We often traversed difficult paths,
some steep and hard to climb,
but we never had the strength
stamina and prowess,
the way Bobbie did when he ran.

It was in the Spring of eighty,
'twas when I first met Bob,
he was working on a contract,
with some government survey mob.

They were working in the Apsley gorge,
planning to build a dam,
giving boost to our electricity needs,
but the country went into recession,
Premier Wran abandoned the plan.

The gorge is at the mouth of the Apsley,
with a thousand metre drop,
the workers had built a track down,
to drive four wheel drives for the job.

Bobbie Beer would always run it,
starting at the top ,
he would run right down to the bottom
and then run back to the top.

Now I know that thousand metre drop,
a sad and lonely spot,
a friend and I moved a huge boulder,
and we pushed it from the top.

It was at that point our white ancestors,
rounded up three hundred men,
full blooded aboriginals,
forced them to jump the gorge.

Now that's a sad sad story,
history books don't tell,
I have a copy of the testament,
of three hundred aboriginal murders,
were our rock boulder silently fell.

But that's another story,
one not taught in Christian schools,
of the death of many black brothers,
'cause they taught us mushroom rules.

Now I am getting away from this story,
the other can wait for another day,
this ones about the wild mountain man,
how he crossed the Simpson desert
a decade or two ago.

Now Bobbie ran from the bottom,
ran back up again
he worked all day with the survey,
ran back out again,
but when the contact folded,
he ran and ran again.

"So raise your glasses,
be of good cheer,
and drink a drink,
to Bobbie Beer."

He ran down a mountain side one day,
disappeared for a week,
in those wild New England ranges,
lived on berries and water from the creeks.

Bobby turned up at the end of June,
on a bitter cold winter's day,
he was wearing untied laced work boots,
football shorts and a torn old shirt.

He came to borrow my paper,
said he was catching a train west,
but I never knew till later,
it was the Simpson desert quest.

"So raise your glasses,
be of good cheer,
and drink a drink,
to Bobbie Beer."

It was all over the newspapers,
the headlines said quite clear,
"A man called Beer run the dry country
the first man to run across."

It was Friday 29th July,1980,
Bobbie Beer crossed our barren land,
in six days,six hours and thirty,
he set a record back then.

Now the township of Birdsville,
quite near the Birdsville track,
had a day of celebration,
the day Bobbie Beer got back.

"So raise your glasses,
be of good cheer,
and drink a drink,
to Bobbie Beer"

He told the newspapers,
of sand hills three storeys high,
how he fell down one,
sprained his ankle and tore his thigh!

Now Bob had stopped drinking,
some ten years before,
he told it straight to the newspapers,
but he drank that day again.

Now other men had tried the feat,
that Bobbie lived to tell,
like Warren Boughton, the scientist,
who knew the desert well.

Boughton crossed the desert ,
in twenty eight days,
but he took a back up crew,
they had plenty of food and water,
dropped from an aeroplane.

So many have tried the desert walk,
many have died as well,
like the Frenchmen Fatin in seventy six,
he was never seen again.

Bobby crossed the desert in record time,
living on water,milk and juice,
he had little back up for his feat,
cause he lost his backup crew.

Dick Smith of electronics fame,
flew his helicopter in,
when he heard about Bob's feat,
he was keen to interview him.

Bobbie didn't want no fame,
he hid back of the Apsley hotel,
there in the dark drinking champagne,
just wanted to be left alone.

Now many others have tried the feat,
to beat old Bobbie's time,
but I think only Pat Farmer did it,
in some new record time.

Oh!the last time I saw Bobbie Beer,
he looked a little worse for wear,
arm in arm with dark Susie Green,
it was at the country music fair.

Well it's been over three decades,
since Bobbie become a folk hero,
I just lost track of him,
on some mountain track I trampled.

Thinking of those days gone by,
as I just tramp along,
and whilst I given up drinking days,
I say to those who do,

"Raise your glasses ,
and remember boys ,
the greatest mountaineer."

"Raise your glasses,
be of good cheer,
drink a drink ,
to Bobbie Beer!"

"To Bobbie Beer."

Creations of the Heart.

In the mind's eye of a dreamer
it's a quest,
like an artist carving images
from stone,
maybe there is nothing on
the other side,
just some crumbling stone.

Still the living can take shape
in mind of man,
springs always new forms
in a heart of stone,
walking on this pathway,
on my way home.

"Perhaps it's why the cowboy
rides the ranges,
burning eyes of coal
in night's log fire,
walking on some lofty hill
at midnight,
seeking out the home
of his desire."

in the mind's eye of the dreamer,
life has meaning,
joins the artist carving forms
new life takes shape,
springs the twinkler of the stars,
new life,new colour,
in the dream there is a reason,
for the stones new shape.

Out of the track of dreams
come words of loving,
like an artist in true form,
carving new shapes,
out of the sea of sound,
springs the music,
in natures stars comes,
the reason for the race.

"Perhaps it's why the cowboy
rides the ranges,
burning eyes of coal
in nights log fire,
walking on some lofty hill
at midnight,
seeking out the home
of his desire."

So what's the use of gifts
if not in service,
bring this creation
to higher power,
the one who created man,
must be awaiting,
to employ his servants,
in this creative hour.

How shall we view
the temple of creation,
sense the obstacles dissolve,
in some sacrifice,
for the working of the mind
a crucifixion,
on the dressed altar,
the mind's creative light.

"Perhaps it's why the cowboy
rides the ranges,
burning eyes of coal
in night's log fire,
walking on some lofty hill
at midnight,
seeking out the home
of his desire."

Many are the instruments
of the searching,
the workings of the mind,
the body soul,
seeking out some magic
of the utterance,
in colour painted clay,
in human stone.

Hear the strings pluck
at the chords,
sound vibrations,
in the brass or reed,
cries the voice,
in hammered tone,
primate dance of body,
a movement of the human soul.

"Perhaps it's why the cowboy,
rides the ranges,
burning eyes of coal,
in nights log fire,
walking on some lofty hill
at midnight,
seeking out the home
of his desire."

A Flaming Star.

Fading memories of old wall posters,
pictured heroes of reckless men,
Davy Crockett on a Tennessee mountain,
with his rifle and coon skin cap!

A hero of a boyhood dreamer,
killing a bear when he was three,
striking out as a leader of men,
fighting for liberty.

John Wayne strode across the scene,
gunfighter of the west,
killing for a just cause,
or some damsel in distress!

He was a leader of wild men,
spoke with a southern drawl,
swaggered across the silver screen,
and opened up the west!

Oh!I walk through fields of clover,
my eyes on the sky above,
with the southern cross above me ,
on a mountain path to love.

Now Jimmy Dean was my idol,
A lone and moody youth,
he mumbled his way through every scene,
but I admired him the best!

Oh, those heroes have long gone,
Davy Crockett at the Alamo,
John Wayne stage left with cancer,
Jimmy Dean with thunderous speed!

Reckless days with my heroes,
with a coon skin cap like Davy,
gun for a John Wayne scene,
playing chicken like James Dean!

Ho! I walk through fields of clover,
my eyes on the sky above,
with the southern cross above me,
on a mountain path to love.

The smell of Californian poppy,
hair brushed with a cockie's comb,
long sideburns for the right effect,
kiss curl to set off the style!

Pink shirt with the collar turned up,
sleeves rolled half way up the arm,
Presley purple stove pipe trousers,
suede shoes with ripple soles!

Kisses in the back seat,
in an FJ Holden car,
listening to a juke box,
music by some in rock star!

I heard the Yellow Rose of Texas,
and big Bonanza gold,
listened to Elvis sing ,
and watched his flaming star!

Ho!I walked through fields of clover,
my eyes on the sky above,
with the southern cross above me,
on a mountain path to love.

Well I read the newspaper,
on the day the music died,
the three amigos of my rhythm,
at the time my way to survive!

Oh! The heroes kept on changing,
other rebels with another cause,
some person ,place or purpose,
to make my life like yours.

Leaders with a cause for justice,
freedom and liberty,
Gandhi and Medgar Evers,
Martin Luther and the Kennedys.

Great speeches of many protests,
swan songs for freedom flies,
assassins bullets are still ringing,
and the children continue to cry.

Oh! I walk through fields of clover,
my eyes on the sky above,
with the southern cross above me,
on a mountain path to love.

New stars are in the making,
flash posters on some kid's wall,
interacting with Facebook and Twitter,
protest marches on every iPhone.

Yeah!the Eagles are still on heart songs,
protest songs of Phil Ochs have faded,
and Dylan's voice is done and dusted,
but he still does songs for love.

Now I'm looking in the mirror ,
on a reckless course of youth,
never took the road less travelled then,
caught up in self abuse!

Yeah! I worked hard for money and power,
tried to be a corporate man,
later married and had children,
true to be the best of them.

Well I gambled too much of the profits,
smoked reefers along the way,
did too much hard core drinking,
until she just left one day.

Yeah!I lost the mother of my kids,
they just went their own way,
i inhaled too many crazy loves,
just tried to get by each day.

Now I walk the road less travelled,
doing the best I can,
being less self opinionated,
helping my fellow man.

Oh!I walk through fields of clover.
my eyes on the sky above,
with the southern cross above me,
on a mountain path to love.

The assassins

Do you hear the words of the poet,
music in the stories he tells,
do you see the signs in the sky now,
how the climate is changing as well.

Do you feel the vibrations of the instruments,
the planes that are dropping your bombs,
can you see the mushroom cloud now,
the killing and maiming that's done.

Do you listen to raw emotion,
the voice in the wildness ride,
have you joined in the unit of legions,
feeding on flesh with the carrion crows.

Cease the bombing and killing of children,
in the name of the father of peace,
give up on the lying and cheating,
call your assassins home for a rest.

Oh! Hash is the drug of deception,
for your killers given the job,
to take out the home of sub culture,
the souls that oppose your mob!

You're moving the souls by the thousands,
to the legions of your all seeing eye,
so please change your war of deception,
just let us the people try.

Now the poet's run out of writing,
his voice has turned to decay,
the words of his songs and his music,
somehow they are fading away.

Presidents and Prime Ministers,
contemplating the hole in the well,
pray to the prince of darkness,
whilst the elephant's still in the room.

Cease the bombing and killing of children,
in the name of the father of peace,
give up the lying and cheating ,
call your assassins home to rest.

Oh! Hash is the drug of deception,
for killers given the job,
to take out the home of sub culture,
the souls that oppose your mob!

Do you take the message of darkness,
the neon light bright in your room,
the all seeing eye of providence,
the dollar bills that sing your tune.

Do you see in the eye of God's country,
prosperity for the land of the free,
is the message still in the star filled banner,
for justice,freedom and liberty.

Yeah! You've killed presidents in their efforts,
to make life better for most,
and you've killed your fair share
of civil rights men,
sweet Jesus, just give up the ghost!

Is it the all seeing eye master,
the architect of the universe,
who set this deal in motion,
is it the four horsemen at work?

Cease the bombing and killing of children,
in the name of the father of peace,
give up the lying and cheating,
call your assassins home to rest.

Oh! Hash is the drug of deception,
for killers given the job,
to take out the home of sub culture,
the souls that oppose your mob!

Shooters and dreamers.

Do you hear the sound of the bell,
the one that rang out for freedom,
claiming liberty throughout the land,
for all Americans?

There was a crack that formed,
in the liberty bell,the first time that it rang,
a warning sign for the road ahead,
for a land of hope and glory.

Did you see the map in forefather's plans,
for a war of independence,
a fight to break the British rule,
to claim a right to freedom?

The shooters and the dreamers,
gave one and all, in a cause of freedom,
through blood and toil,sweat and tears,
they carved an American nation.

Do you recall the simple folk,
who worked to build the nation,
claimed their birthright,one for all,
tilled the soil and built the cities.

Did you see the dust of a wagon train,
crossing the barren land,
with dreamy eyes hitched to a star,
the folk who built the nation.

Do you remember the Alamo.
when Santa Anna with his men,
crossed over the Rio Grande,
to reclaim the lone star land?

The shooters and dreamers,
gave one and all ,in a cause of freedom,
through blood and toil,sweat and tears,
they carved an American nation.

We grew in their dreams and folk legend,
Davy Crockett and Jim Bowie,
stood toe to toe with a small band,
fought and died defending the land.

It was the time of legends,
the lawless and law men,
guns to get what they wanted,
guns to keep the peace back then.

Do you recall the many tales,
the stories of great lawmen,
the feats of Wyatt Earp and Doc Holliday,
in the gunfight at O.K. Corral.

The shooters and dreamers,
gave one and all,in a cause for freedom,
through blood and toil,sweat and tears,
they carved an American nation.

What of the feats of wild women,
the shooters like Calamity Jane,
who rode like the wind on horseback,
and could shoot with the best of them.?

Maybe you remember Annie Oakley,
the master of all with a gun,
no one could out draw or out shoot her,
she always got her target in one.

Do you remember still,the civil war,
the fight for cause of freedom,
to unite the country as one,
with liberty and justice for all?

Shooters and dreamers,
gave one and all, in cause of freedom,
through blood and toil,sweat and tears,
they carved an American nation.

How did the cause to rally round the flag,
at the end of a bloody war,
claim the birthright of a nation
stars and stripes for one and all?

Jesse James held up the trains,
and robbed a bank or two,
lived in Missouri a double life,
as Thomas Howard a business dude.

Oh!A dirty little coward,
shot poor old Mister Howard,
shot him in the back
and laid poor Jesse in his grave.

You've heard of wild men ,
Butch Cassidy and the Sundance kid,
they caught a bullet for their efforts,
holding up banks was the death of them.

Shooters and dreamers,
gave one and all,in the cause of freedom,
through blood and toil,sweat and tears,
they carved an American nation.

Then there was William Mc Carty,
better know as Billy the kid,
no man could out shoot or outdraw him,
Pat Garret the lawman did.

Many a wild cowboy,
in the foundation of the west,
tried to shoot their way to fame,
but the lawmen beat the best.

There where those of fame,
entertainment was their game,
like Buffalo Bill's Wild West show,
Annie Oakley was the main attraction.

Shooters and dreamers,
gave one and all,in the cause of freedom,
through blood and toil,sweat and tears,
they carved an American nation.

Tom Mix gave up his outlaw ways,
went on to movie making,
he was the hero of the silent screen,
a banner for the best of the nation.

Well we've had two world wars,
Americans came to the cause,
fought for the right of their fellow man,
and the freedom it would bring.

So much blood flowed under the flag,
so many war heroes now dead,
gun slingers fighting for the land of the free,
shooters and dreamers now dead.

When the movies turned to talkies,
John Wayne was the hero back then,
he was the hero of the west,
as he swaggered across the screen.

So many wild men followed,
stories of misspent youth and men,
James Dean went out in a ball of flame,
easy rider was an American dream.

Shooters and dreamers,
gave one and all,in the cause of freedom.
through blood and toil,sweat and tears,
they carved an American nation.

Well civil rights leaders and presidents,
all killed in the name of peace,
never got the laurel wealth they deserved,
thou they died for an ultimate cause.

Now the world is awash with the shooters,
killing for a just cause,
and the world of entertainment,
lost in the dreamers pursuits.

Do you hear the sound of a bell,
the one that rung out for freedom,
claiming liberty throughout the land,
for all Americans.

There was a cracked that formed,
in the liberty bell,the first time that it rang,
a warning sign for the road ahead,
for a land of hope and glory.

Oh! The liberty bell rang only once,
as far as the records tell,
the nation built another to ring again,
we now wonder for whom it tolls.

Shooters and dreamers.
gave one and all,in the cause of freedom.
through blood and toil,sweat and tears,
they carved an American nation.

The last stockman.

Now old Barney was my granddad,
he had many a tale to tell,
some were happy and sad ones,
others were just fables!

He told of a sad sad story,
of an old stockman name of Ned,
it was in the wild Mallee country,
about the day the stockman died.

Well the sun dawn broke slowly,
on that misty dust dull dawn,
spreading eastern rays,
across the sluggish land.

It was Ned's last dreaming morning,
on his final cattle trail,
were the sun shot a flaming pathway,
to view the sand peaks blazed.

The bleary eyed stockmen,
were saddling up to break camp,
they were holding on to their horses,
to bridle them and saddle.

They were just starting the muster,
to drive the cattle across the land,
finished their last tea and damper,
to let out across the plain.

Old Ned stepped from the saddle,
and he went when nature called,
squat down by a Mallee scrub,
it was the only tree about.

Old Ned yelled out a holler,
"The bastards bit me ass",
as the cunning brown snaked hid,
neath the tree that evil asp!

Well Ned he cursed and grumbled,
as he got up on his horse,
he had treated the wound as best he could,
who could bandage a bitten ass.

Oh! They drove the cattle all that day,
till Ned called out to Barnie,
"See that old tree up ahead,
I'd like to cut a branch off,
make a hook and sink the sun"

Barney,my old granddad, in a joke,
said in a matter a fact way,
"I'd rather cut a Fork,
prop up the sun for longer,
finish the drove and collect my pay."

To the south the sand hills
were a blaze,
to the west a bridle path,
led to a bluff,
and to the side of the first hill,
a place to camp at last!

It was a perfect campsite,
not far from the drive stop,
near tea trees on a pathway,
were eucalypts grew a lot.

"Well lift me from the saddle" cried Ned,
"old friend I am on my last,
you did good to guide my horse,
now the asp's poison has taken its grasp."

He smiled as he lay their dying,
remembering times that past,
he was in his dreaming of his times
in the saddle,
telling an old tale of the past.

"Oh! I remember a glowing morning,
out on the gleaming grass,
when we watched our cool tobacco clouds,
watched the white wreaths pass."

"We sat loosely in the saddle,
as we railed the cattle in yards,
rang the fire of our stock whips raging,
and our fiery run of hooves."

"We were a glowing band of drovers,
as we rode the sun dried land,
the flint stone echoed the ranges,
were the cattle stampede rang,"

"Close behind them through the tea tree,
through the golden timbered fern,
beneath the weeping willows,
we trapped them in the gorge."

"Yeah! We were the best of men" cried Ned ,
In his dying breath,
you were riding the chestnut Barney,
and me the old grey horse."

"We emptied flaming six shooter,
rode the chestnut and the grey,
and we cracked our whips
till the steers were done,
man to man we won the day."

Now old Ned began to pray,
as they watched him slip away,
so they buried him by an old gum tree,
under rocks to keep dingoes at bay.

Barney returned to the place,
were Ned was bitten by the asp,
he turned over every rock and stick,
till he found that snake at last.

So He loaded up his shotgun,
and he blew the snake away,
granddad always wore snake skin boots,
from that very day.

Now the wheat grows where once was cattle,
no more drovers on the plain,
long haul trucks carry them to market,
and dams where once there was rain.

There blooms tea trees and the wattle,
were once they could not grow,
there are trains now full of iron ore,
were the cattle men once rode the plain.

Oh! The deep blue skies wax dusty,
tall grass grows on the plain,
were the smoky sinking shadows,
hide the sleeping sunlight rays.

Let me slumber in the hollow,
were the white blossoms wave,
with never a stone or rail to fence me in,
put bush flowers upon my grave.

Just for now let me live in the sunshine,
walk in the wind and the rain,
carry my knapsack and tucker bag,
to see were the last stockman was laid.

'Cause I guess when the time will come,
like it does for every man,
I will end up with Barnly my granddad,
and I go were most men go.

Section 5-Sahagun to Leon

Leaving the vast 'Tierra de Compoa' behind,the pilgrim continues across more cereal and grain crop fields to reach the plateau of Leon.Along the way the pilgrim will pass the pretty village of Reliegos and take the 'Via Traiana' trail past more crop fields and on to the first sign of industrial activity approaching the city.

Leon,the historic capital of the kingdom in the middle ages is an historic enclave on the pilgrim's route to Santaigo de Compostela. The Pulchra Leonina in the Leon cathedral is the 'Sistine Chapel' of spanish architecture.Gaudi's neo-gothic Casta de Botines and the old 'Hospital de San Marcos' add to the luxury and decor.

The cottages,museums food outlets and character of the locals is like a vista of a poor mans Paris.

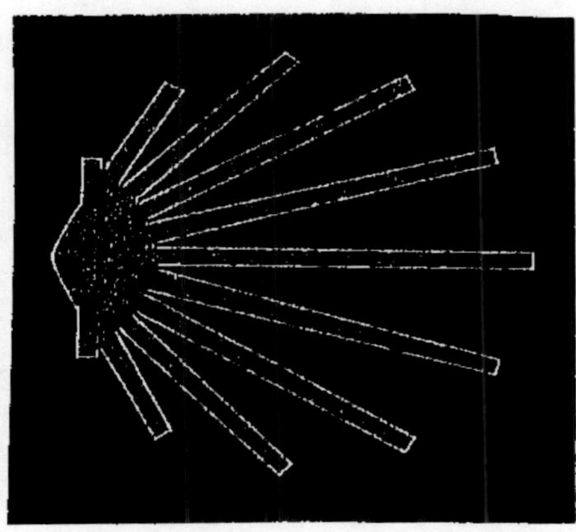

Section 5-WORDS FOR MY BROTHERS

ARCHIE ROACH

DROUGHT PRAYER

NO LONGER IN A BUBBLE

THE MAKERS OF DREAMS

WORDS TO A FRIEND

HANDS

OBSOLETE ANT?

SOAKING UP THE MORROW

MISSION MOUNTAIN

DREAMTIME

Section 5-Words for My Brothers

"Humility is my table,respect is my garment,
empathy is my food and curiosity is my drink.
As for Love,it has a thousand names and
is by my side at every window".

-Tariq Ramadan,The Quest for Meaning.

"Random thoughts of childhood and my dark brothers of my dreaming ,making woomeras and listening to the sounds of the bull roarer,cutting corkwood,living on the edge of freedom, freewheeling on my push bike,watching my best friend drown and my black brother raise his body from the ocean floor......"

"Letting go of past joy and pain,the things of childhood,creating a mantra in my head,thinking of how to help a friend of the way,mindful of the world and our lot in it,thinking of tomorrow,a reason for living,walking the mountain ranges of the Camino wishing it would rain,talking to God above and seeming to get no immediate answers........"

"Returning to the dreamtime of my black brothers,smelling the dry dust of the road,wishing it would rain,walking my Camino......"

"It is the search for love that is my course,travelling this lonely road,back to my heart......."

Listening to Archie Roach.

Who can explain
the strain on your face,
knowing your burdens
you carry for race,
It's like some itching
underneath the skin.

We were just kids then,
we did not understand,
nature's link to the native man.
learning how to throw a boomerang!

Being skilled in killing with a spear,
using the woomera!
sending messages over land,
bull roarers singing in the air!

How could we understand,
we stood in segregated classes,
life was a prism back then,
coloured in rose coloured glasses.

We sat together in class,
there was no black or white,
only shades of grey,
we all took a caning from the nuns,
bound by a code of rugby league.

We were the champion team,
white boys were the pigs,
black boys had the lightning speed,
we won the games and went back to our race.

We kissed the girls in the back row ,
oblivious to our heroes
on the movie screen,
Popcorn and ice cream at interval.

Whilst the black boys ate the Jaffas ,
we rolled to them in the front row,
It was the only place they where allowed to be,
a little too close to the screen.

It was Slim Dusty who sang on the radio.
Dave Sands was the champ of the fighting team,
Jimmy Sharman was beating his boxing drum,
and the kids at burnt bridge where a stolen generation.

Jimmy Little,like Slim Dusty,
was the pride of our nation,
and Archie Roach was
just some young boy's dream.

We climbed trees for birds nesting,
collecting our batch,
learnt to blow them,
before they could hatch.

We killed lizards for pleasure,
smoked cain when in leisure,
cut cork wood for money,
caught fish when in need.

We were the kids of the drinking,
fire dancing out of mind,
the fights and the poverty
It just seemed right.

We were just kids,
we did not understand,
the pride of the working class,
nature's link to the native man!

Mapped lines upon our faces tell,
of old folk dead and gone,
children carry on oblivious,
to the the life that is now gone.

We no longer have Slim Dusty,
singing his travelling songs,
Jimmy Sharmans gone to heaven too,
with his boxing troupe tagging along.

Dave Sands is just a memory,
like so many etched in stone,
and the kids of Burnt Bridge are still crying now,
old men not knowing their home.

And the sound of Jimmy Little,
no longer a glory tune,
and the sound of Jimmy Little,
no longer a glory tune.

Black eyes are still showing the strain,
tears rising up to a tune,
women are out there dancing
afraid to stay back in their room

Who can explain,
the strain on your face,
knowing the burdens,
you carry for race,
It's like some itching,
underneath the skin!

Listening to Archie Roach,
singing the country blues
Oh!listening to Archie Roach,
singing the country blues.

Drought prayer.

Oh ancient sage of eons past
and cosmic overview,
gazing upon majestic star:
the potter planet earth.

Fire and smoke,sage and cedar,
sweet grass,tobacco too.
fire and smoke,sage and cedar,
we come to honour you.

Meteoric eyes of heaven sent,
beneath the southern cross,
searching out the Stone Age land,
Australia's continent,

Fire and smoke,tallow and wattle,
ghost gums,grey and blue,
fire and smoke,tallow and wattle,
we come to honour you.

Dusty plains of redden earth,
stretch out across the plain,
broken by mountains of blue,
through sun drenched haze,
and shadows of rain.

Rainbow clouds drift over the divide,
as roars a distant thunder,
warning promised sheets of rain,
to a dry land down under.

Fire and smoke,sage and cedar,
sweet grass,tobacco too,
fire and smoke,sage and cedar,
we come to honour you.

The coastal fringe of white sand beach,
tall timbers and green grass,
kept alive by ocean mist,
that drift along their path,
are but a morsel to a mouse,
we pray the drought won't last.

Fire and smoke,sage and cedar,
sweet grass ,tobacco too,
fire and smoke,sage and cedar,
we come to honour you.

Blind eyes of man,once only dark,
join green eyes grey and blue,
creations pray for our parched earth,
crystal to light the view,rains to blossom nature's way
and colour our eyes too.

The native man with ancient hand,
raised to hide the sun,
casts dark eyes across the land,
he prays in ancient tongue,
for rains renewal to starving earth,
dried gullies and parched streams.

The murmur of the bull roarer,
calls tribesmen from afar,
to play the didgeridoo,
for rainbow clay.
blind skins have come to share,
a dance in coloured skin paint way,
a rhythm in hot air.

The sound of movement in spirit earth,
a prayer to God of rain,
to trust that in their offering,
the skies will flood the plain.

Fire and smoke,sage and cedar,
fresh grass,tobacco too,
fire and smoke ,sage and cedar,
we come to honour you.

Fire and smoke,tallow and wattle,
ghost gums grey and blue,
fire and smoke,tallow and wattle,
we come to honour you.

No longer in a bubble.

There's no need for explanation,
turn your heart to sing the blues,
waste no time in vain lit glories,
you have nothing left to lose.

Give up,living in your ego,
flame is dying in your head,
turn away from vain lit pleasure,
live the sacredness instead.

Let the scales fall from your eyes,
hear the sounds within your voice,
touch the nature of your longing,
step on in and out to choice.

Feel the magic of your lifeline,
and the cold that lays within,
you're no longer in a bubble,
on the outside looking in,

So I'm on a road less travelled,
with the sun upon my back,
and my eye upon a moonbeam,
as I stretch out for a nap!

And I sing a song for youth,
It's a memory coming back,
of the joys we felt in childhood,
with a knapsack on my back.

You're no longer in a bubble,
there is no need to explain,
it will make no sense to anyone,
those still living in the game.

There's no cause to explain action,
no need to toll a bell,
just free falling in the moment,
somewhere between heaven and hell.

No longer living in a bubble,
we are the music and the dream,
wandering by a lonely sea shore,
sailing on a desolate stream.

Letting go of earthly wisdom,
staring into the pale moon's face,
just not being in a hurry,
life is not a race.

Listening to the voice of silence,
hand it over to Godly quest,
living life unto the fullest,
it's up to you in willingness.

"Bright lights come and go,
playing blue songs on my radio;
Shadows still appear in the house tonight,
ghosts have come in from the past,oh yeah,
all those ghosts that keep coming back,
sliding through the walls and my window...."

-Annie Lennox lyrics.

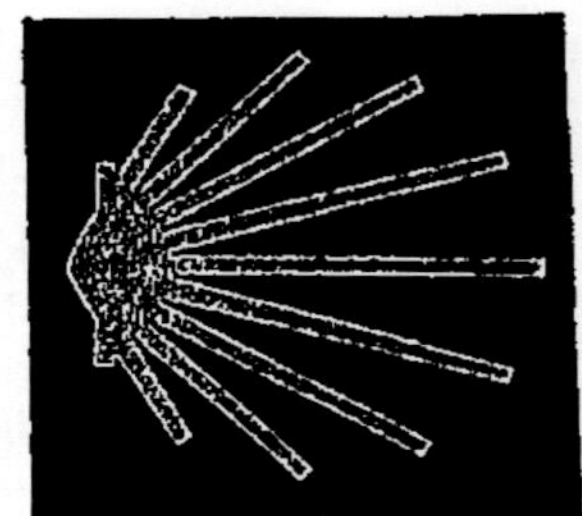

The makers of dreams.

Now if you listen carefully
you will get it in your drift,
it's all within our music,
and any chorus riff!

We are the music makers,
the tellers of our dreams,
shattering the sounds of silence,
at least thats how it seems.

Our quest moves to a beat,
you must stay in tune,
listen to the lyrics,
as we cry out to the moon!

Take the journey inward,
the ancient way within,
you may catch it if you listen,
it's the chorus riff within.

We are the atlas eaters,
a voice for the dreamers of dreams,
within a world lost and forsaken,
singing its death knell it seems.

Our quest is to follow our star,
to fashion and change with our sound
we've lyrics and music to measure,
to turn the universe all around.

We master the words of the dreamer,
helped by the Master it seems,
tune makers of the trampled,
guides to our youthful dreams!

We are the music makers,
the tellers of tales,
so it seems,
we've music to play
words for today,
nations are animal themes.

"The lion roars in the jungle,
bears free to roam about,
whilst the herd looks
to the king of beast for truth.

The king has lost his crown,
for the herd is at a loss,
while the king just sits,
pawing at the ground.

The kiwi is travelling with sheep now,
the kangaroos keeping up pace,
elephant long on the memory,
the owl has a scowl on his face!

The lion and the pride,
search the sky now,
trusting the past may return,
hoping against all reason,
the Eagle will once more soar.

Watch for the signs of the changing,
when the animals all gather as one,
some will be held in cages,
whilst the bear is angry and proud!

And the rest with some fear,
search the sky now,
whilst the Eagle is soaring about,
and the Dragon keeps wearing the crown!

We are the animals too,
we are the prophets of truth,
we are the prophets of doom!
don't let it get to you too much,
we've time to freedom as one.

Now if you listen carefully,
you will get it in your drift,
it's all within our music,
and any chorus riff!

We are the music makers,
the tellers of our dreams,
shattering the sounds of silence,
at least that's how it seems.

We are The prophets of truth
we are the prophets of doom,
take note of the lyrics,
it's all in the animal tunes.

Words to a friend.

Take it easy,

so they say,
let go let God,
leave yesterday ,
It's better that way!

You are not alone,
friends are everywhere,
get a grip,
take it easy,
It's no time for despair!

The fish are still swimming in the ocean,
the birds are still flying in the air!

Take it easy,
life is unfolding,
It's better this way,
cruising within the moment,
staying within the day!

Don't try and understand it,
let it take its hold,
give up being on the ball,
come in from the cold!

It's all a great mystery,
no need to pretend,
live in the experience,
let your God be your friend!

Stop trying to hold on,
controlling the whole thing,
life is just unfolding
beginning to the end!

The fish are still swimming in the ocean,
the birds are still flying in the air!

Just be and let be,
live and let live,
no agenda to value,
give in and you'll live.

live in the moment,
love,really live!

If you are sad,then be sad,
feel lonely,take it in,
feels are just feelings,
just begin to begin.

Shout your tears to the hill tops,
cry out,don't hold back,
you'll be o.k. now,
give in to begin,
your back on track!

The fish are still swimming in the ocean,
the birds are still flying in the air!

“And you shall seek me,and find me,
when you search with all your heart. "

-Jeremiah 29:13

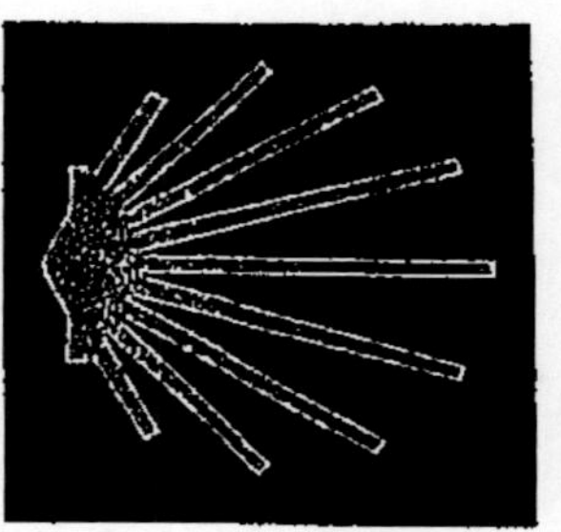

Hands

There are many hands working,
many more at play
many more that suffer,
some held up to prayer.

Some are raised in anger,
whilst others fire guns,
those bent on destruction,
hands for their kingdom come!

Let's all join hands together,
in loving kindness way,
justice,truth and freedom,
our hands will show the way.

So take the hand of friendship,
the one right next to you,
holding hands together,
our hearts in hand renew!

There are hands held out in hunger,
many more that show despair,
whilst some enjoy the freedom,
good food ,shelter and fresh air!

There are hands who know the good life,
of money,power and means,
flying down the highways,
in their great limousines!

Let's all join hands together,
in loving kindness way,
justice ,truth and freedom,
poor hands will show the way.

So take the hand of freedom,
the one right next to you,
holding hands together,
our hearts with hands renew!

There are hands paint landscapes,
those that write and toil,
some who save the environment,
whilst others till the soil.

There are hands who point in judgement,
where open hands accuse,
those bent on a guilt plea,
whilst other hands abuse.

There are hands who give with love,
whilst others self abuse,
those bent of self destruction,
whilst others stand accused.

Let's all join hands together,
put away the guns,
laugh and play and sing aloud,
let the past go down with the sun.

and in the morning glory,
let us all hold hands and pray,
for black and white and brindle,
our hands can show the way.

Let all join hands together,
my brothers, you know the way.

Obsolete Ant ?

Wow!

Now this ant has left the ground,
he at last sees up and down,
but to his fellow ants,
he's just one of them,
maybe he still has a role to play,
work for the state or just for pay?

Oh!

Now the ant has left the ground,
left behind his cross and crown,
just a small poetic ant,
pacing forward and back in chance,
eking out his daily bread,
no longer living in his head.

Ha!

Now the ant has left the ground,
obsolete to his fellow ants,
he waits his ultimate demise,
no more a victim or hero in disguise,
outward looking in,inward being wise,
listening to the message of his creator.

Hark!

Now the ant has left the ground,
he has a quest but not a crown,
listen,wait,don't make a sound,
hear the heart beat of his fellow ants,
there's a purpose whilst still on earth.
an ultimate plan of the universe.

Pax!

In godly steps he takes the plunge,
the inward journey's opening up,
what can he be but the best for him,
a recognition to his fellow ants,
witness to his and their cause,
saying little but doing a lot.

Daily Bread!

Now the ant has left the ground,
pacing forward and back again,
seeing up and seeing down
being the best that he can,
he is not obsolete,
listening to his fellow ants!

Now the ant has left the ground,
the cups half empty,the cups half full,
a taste of water,a little bread,
all an ant needs to live on,
the quest he has to follow a star,
being the best example to his fellow ants!

Ants are smart,some are dumb,
making a living or making none,
there's the rich and the poor,
for those in health ,others are sick,
whilst some are famous ,others not,
each has a purpose in a bigger plot!

Insight!

It's not too late to leave the ground.
seeing up and seeing down,
feeding fellow ants your daily bread,
no longer living in your head,
no ant in truth is obsolete,
we ants must do what we must do!

Now!

Every ant can go forward and back,
it's more than a function,it's a living fact,
it's not just nature,more than fresh air,
looking up and looking down,
the ultimate design is a Godly plan!

Nothingness!

The poetic ant goes forward and back,
still in silence up and down,
nil in glory,no more the crown,
conscious of his mortal lot,
bound for glory in a heavenly plot,
tolls the bell,ticks the clock!

Make the most of what you've got,
take on the truth,let go the lies,
remove the mask that hides your eyes,
heavens gate is not a disguise ,
learning to be wise for the ultimate prize,
saying little,doing a lot!

Epilogue!

This little ant goes forward and back,
looking up and looking down,
living with the inner ant,
mindful of nothing before time began,
pen and paper poetic ant,
write it down before it's forgot!

Amen to that,exit stage.........Right!

Soaking in the morrow

It's said that a road less travelled
may heal a broken heart,
blind faith in a God of light,
to lead you through the dark.

A friend in times uncertain,
where courage masks fear,
stepping out to what may be,
will overcome your tears.

Gazing on a starry night,
soaking in the morrow.

A life that's been broken needs
time to repair,
alone with nature's glory,
bush birds and clean fresh air,
touched by sun drenched rain and shadow.

Gazing on a starry night,
soaking in the morrow

Go gently sleepy broken heart,
let go the pain and sorrow,
these things have passed,
like passing friends,
for new horizons follow.

Yes!all that was in yesterday,
will vanish in the shadow,
gazing on a starry night,
soaking in the morrow!

There is a new life drawing,
yours will never be the same
new love,joy and friendship
will help you free the pain.

Being stung in ageless wisdom
has come through bitter sorrow,
gazing on a starry night,
soaking in the morrow.

"Life is either a daring adventure or nothing at all."

-Helen Keller.

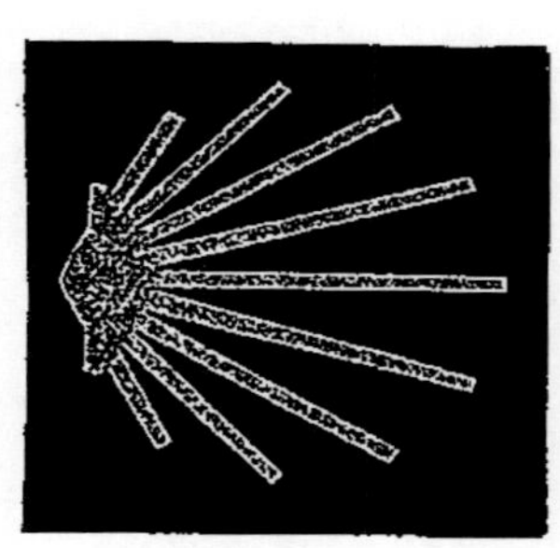

Mission mountain.

There's a track to mission mountain,
it's the pathway of my dreams,
a way along the byway,
of valleys,hills and streams.

An oath to Godly purpose,
in the spirit plain above,
a reason for my living,
on a road to endless love.

There's a track in old Barque country,
were I found my way,
with tent,knapsack and tucker bag,
I waltzed the Matilda way.

Walking the Spanish highlands,
on the Camino,
walking the Spanish highlands,
on the Camino.

So sweet muse of mission mountain,
the source of light and love,
lead on this weary traveller,
too tramp the path to love.

There is nature's endless wonder,
by valleys ,hills and streams,
bringing all now to reality,
not just in my dreams.

There's a track in old Barque country,
were I found my way,
with tent,knapsack and tucker bag,
I waltzed the Matilda way.

Walking the Spanish highlands,
on the Camino,
walking the Spanish highlands,
on the Camino.

Dreamtime.

Awakened to the dreamtime,
wonder in a daze,
called by the love sound cicada,
and a far of kookaburra!

Dazed in a sunlight blaze,
of where it all began,
telling a dreamtime tale,
of universe and man.

Viewing the seep of silver sky,
colours rainbow too,
caught in the tale of serpent fire
and the far off sound of a bird!

Swimming with fish to feel their fear,
sliding with crocodile,
slithering and hissing like a snake,
watching a pale moon rising!

Dreaming an ancient story,
tribesmen must respect,
one man's painted dream,
imagined in the telling,
or playing an instrument!

Feeling the dry earth on my feet,
hearing the drum in my heart,
seeing through ancient eyes,
the beginning and end,
at the start!

Yes! we are the music makers,
we are the makers of dreams,
wandering by lone sea breakers,
sitting by desolate streams:

World losers and world forsakers,
on whom the pale moon gleams,
we are the movers and shakers
of the world forever it seems!

Section 6- Leon to Ponferrada

The Camino from Leon to Mazarife is pretty flat and easy. One walks through fields of grain,corn,potatoes and apple orchards along footpaths and dirt tracks to the prettiest village on the Camino,Hospital de Orbigo. Here the pilgrim will cross the famous 'Puente de Origo' bridge with the distant scene of the Leon mountains as the pretty hilltop city of Astorga ,the capital of Margateria is reached.The 'pink' cathedral,the Gaudi-designed episcopal palace and the city walls are unforgettable as are the local chocolates.

Gradually the pilgrim makes the way to the Leon mountains and El Bierzo region surrounded by bloom,heather and oak. The climb to 'Mount Irago with the company of the bloom and heather is a stark contrast to the Iron Cross on the mountain top and a good point to contemplate before descending to the lush area of the El Bierzo.A stay in the mountain village of Acebo is a peaceful place before entry to the city of Ponferrada,

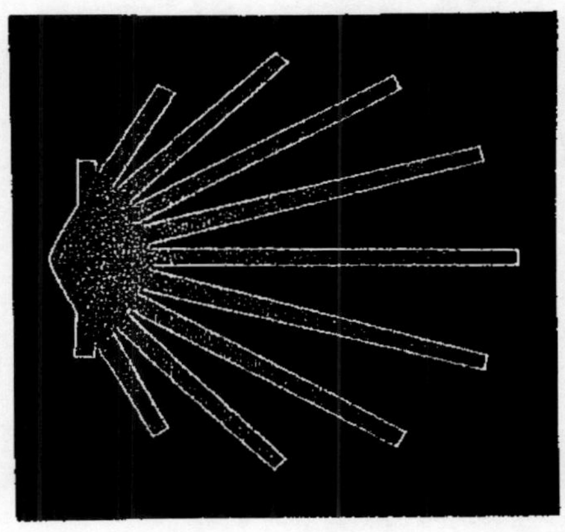

"The stumbling blocks to my Camino were eased by the pilgrims I met along the way"

Section 6- Lessons in healing.

"I'm going to smile and make you think I am happy,I'm going to laugh,so you don't see me cry,I'm going to let go in style,and even if it kills me-I'm going to smile".

-Anonymous

When we have longed to reach a goal for many years and finally get there after many battles and hardships,we expect to feel content,fulfilled and at peace.Yet,all too often,the opposite happens,and we cannot understand why,having climbed to the top of the mountain,feeling a great sense of achievement and contentment, some how on our return to the valley floor below ,the vista seems grey,bleak and without hope. Whether it is a position of worldly responsibility or the acquisition of material objects,so many of us are driven,or so it seems to be,by the need to have something,to win something,to gain something,to be somebody other than self. Yet our journey reveals a secret of the human heart.It is not the prize,but the struggle,which makes us feel alive and to which we offer our greatest love and commitment. And,although we are reluctant to admit it,it is the struggle which bring out the best in us.

My pattern was of high success,a battle for recognition and wealth,a slide into misery,physical illness and depression and a darkness of the soul, seeming now unimaginable. Like a knight of old with symbol of fire and sword, I took up the mantle ,full of courage, aspiration and will ,despite hardship,to win the great fight.What does one do with this powerful,impetuous,noble spirit when one's cause for fighting is dead? The fruit has withered on the vine,some of the branches are now dead but do I still hang around with words of discernment,doing my little bit to water the remaining vines that still may bear fruit.

Yes,it is my responsibility to be there to provide waters of nature to invigorate my offspring but only if they are open to it. We as human beings need to first fulfil our individual ambitions and then to recognise that we belong to a community at large and to make some contribution to the greater whole in order to allow life to flow within once again.

A time comes when we contemplate what the struggle has all been for and for who and what it really serves. Perhaps it's time to plant another mustard seed ,nurture it and with the help of a higher power in nature,be there to help it grow.

"Nowhere can man find a queiter and more untroubled retreat than in his own soul."

-Marcus Aurelius.

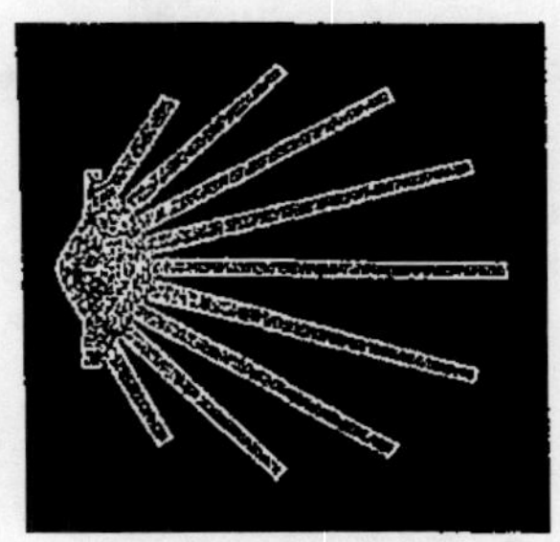

SECTION 6-THE LESSON IN HEALING

BUTTERFLY.

SOUL SHATTERED MIRACLE.

TO CHRIST ASCENDING.

THE END OF THE RAINBOW.

Butterfly.

Letting go is the answer,
from the darkness to the light,
rainbow dreams fall away now,
caught up in a starry night.

Silky magic weaving wonder,
diamonds sparkle not yet seen,
waking from some sleepy hollow,
cocoon caterpillar dream.

Mushroom mind bred in darkness,
slowing waking to the light,
dawning on a strange reflection,
Illuminated by the light.

Butterfly,
bathed in splendour,
fluttering wings are riding high,
like a moth drawn to the flame,
all those colours of my dreams.

Drink nectar from the flowers,
fly on high towards the flame,
living out your life cycle,
touched by the light,
you'll burn out soon.

Blackness of the mind awaken,
silence mystery of the age,
words are but forked lightning,
an expression on the page,
all the colours of my dreams.

Silky magic carry me now,
on your magic rainbow scene,
living out the words of reason,
in a technicolor dream,
grasping words just fade away.

Living in the light of day now,
all the colours melting to one,
of the daylight wing my way now,
flying back towards the sun,
silent shadows dying light

Butterfly,
bathed in splendour,
flutter wings are riding high,
like a moth drawn to the flame,
all the colours of my dreams.

Drinking nectar from the flowers,
fly on high towards the flame,
living out your life cycle,
touched by the light,
you'll burn out soon.

There is purpose in a cocoon,
in a poets forging tune,
rhymes a reason for the silk
and the worm that makes it breath,
butterfly colours my dreams.

So I tramped the road less travelled
on a lonely dusty path,
heart beats to my own drummer,
silent master soothes my pain,
as I seek the light again.

You are all that is the wonder,
the lover of my soul,
handing me a constant torment,
expressions of a lover's mind,
as I wing my way to light.

Butterfly,
bathed in splendour,
flutter wings are riding high,
like a moth drawn to the flame,
all this colours of my dreams.

Drinking nectar from the flowers,
fly on high towards the flame,
living out your life's cycle,
touched by light,
you'll burn out soon.

To Christ Ascending.

So many roads we travel,
seeking our own will,
in tune with sunlight and shadow,
no time in peace to be still,
paying lip service to you.

Not knowing who we pray too,
we pray.

Then the living pull us back,
shattered loss of love,
loss of living will,
time stands still in darkness,
blinding fear saps our skill.

Not knowing who we pray too,
we pray.

Reaching out like Paul for sight,
so much terror still,
doubting Thomas wanting proof,
missing now the worldly wisdom,
yearning for return of youth,
we dream to do your will.

Not knowing who we pray too,
we pray.

It matters not in truth or fable,
prophet,sage upon the cross,
in the manifest of history,
your spirit wins the toss.

Not knowing who we pray too,
we pray.

In this truth we are ascending,
so we sing your glory be,
in the heart of doubts believers,
thy kingdom come,
thy trinity!

Oh! Let us see the light eternal,
courage in your love we'll be,
fools for Christ,
our lives uplifted,
in your will eternally!

It's never too late to mend our ways.

Soul shattered miracle

We are but shattered pieces,
of a mirror in the void,
a universal reflection,
of the light in the darkest scene.

A mirror of a prism,
beaming visions of illumination,
a dull reflection of the glory,
in thought,in word,in deed,

The great awakening of the cosmos,
as in chaos it evolves,
to some orderly existence,
in a sound that we don't know.

Man cannot recreate,
the mirror of creation,
but we can conceive,
some order out of chaos!

This Godly world's a miracle,
a dream beyond belief,
in unity of purpose,
all things are possible.

In a one world united,
were love rains hate is dead,
the world's wounds can be mended,
so let the miracle begin.

This Godly world's a miracle,
as oneness we are God,
in unity of purpose,
all things are possible!

The end of the rainbow

The sun's rays flash dark curtains open,
fiery eyes herald the sun,
morning star on fading moon drops,
rain in mystic colours run,
directing dreamers to their gold,
somewhere beyond the rainbows beam,

Stumbling dreamers,leading souls;
turning back from clouded night,
in your age of youth and wisdom,
you seek strength,both brave and bold.

When your body loses strength,
you are overcome by fear,
life's boldness no longer beckons,
for in truth you're growing old,

Yet you seek the seed of wonder,
from beneath the rainbow's gold,
chains are breaking,freedom's dawning,
as you tramp the mountain's path,

Climb the highest peak you can find,
stumbling down the vale below,
the pot of gold keeps on moving,
as a new rainbow unfolds.

Seek your God in desolate places,
that's what only we fools do,
stay a while in spirit stillness,
the pot of gold inside of you!

Section 7-Pontferrrada to Sarria

Memories of the impressive Templars castle in Ponferrada fade as the pilgrim walks in the lush pastures of the El Bierzo nestled in the mountains.Tastes of exquiste cured meats and delicious cherries from the local villages and visit to the garden of Iglesia de Santiago at Villafranca and the 'Forgiveness Gate', Puerta del Pardon, nourish the body and the heart.

The way follows the valley via the Valcarca river before a challenging ascent to the ranges of 'Os Ancares and Sierra do Courel' passing through the Ranadoiro mountains and across the Alto do Polo descending into the village of Triacastela.

The 'San Xil' Camino offers scenery that fortifies the pilgrim's spirit,whilst the narrow forest track as an optional way slices through typical Galician oak woods.An alternate route to Sarria through Samos and the impressive monastery is perhaps the first town in the region where the pilgrim can enjoy the delicacy of freshly cooked octopus.Walking across the valley of the river and following the path of the river to Sarria is a wonderful acknowledgement that man cannot do what nature provides.

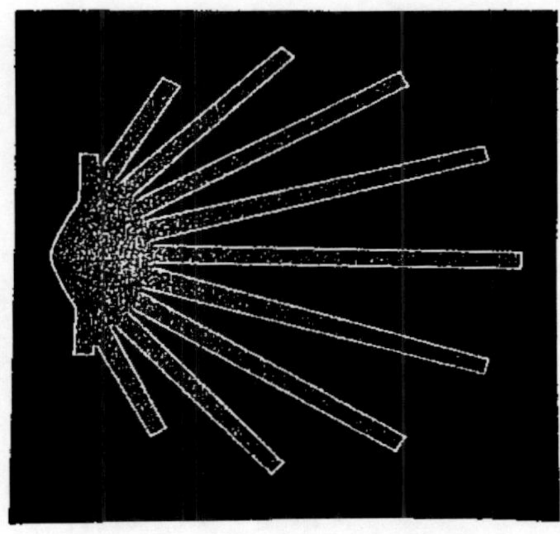

987 310232
600 471897
ESPECIALIDAD EN:
CECINAS
LOMOS
CHORIZOS
SALCHICHONES...
ELABORACIÓN ARTESANAL
PEREGRINO · ALBERGUE

SECTION 7-POEMS IN THE HEALING

FAITH IS THE BIRD

OLD MAN AT THE SIDEWALK CAFE.

ON CONTEMPLATING RUBENS' NUDE.

REGAINING CONFIDENCE.

"Faith is the bird........"

There was once a broken little bird
who lost the gift of flight,
or so it seemed in its darkest hour,
the wind was not quite right,

How could the air in storm or mist
help a bird to flight?
how could he sing to other birds,
for there was none in sight?

So there he was alone and lost
in sadness and in doubt,
it was to this little bird,
what life was all about.

Going deep within its agony,
our feathered friend rehearsed,
searching down memory lane,
praying not to be bound to earth,
was he not made to fly and soar,
why was it in reverse?

To search to chance some carefree way,
to jump and trust to fly,
our bird searched for an easy route,
so that this bird might fly.

But in the scary moments,
the unbelief prevailed,
so he began to doubt the truth
for flight to bird was fable!

In time of course the renewed bird,
believed he was all right,
climbed to the highest mountain top,
there to attempt to flight.

So with courage before reason,
he jumped from this great height,
and with the help of wind and air,
this bird returned to flight,

Footnote:
"Faith is the bird that feels the height
and sings while the dawn's still dark."
- Lagore.

Old man at the sidewalk cafe.

There's an old man,
at the sidewalk cafe,
drinking his coffee slow,
just sitting there taking it easy;
no longer on the go!

Is that the old man
who made a fortune,
the hero of Big Dome and co?
didn't he see it crumble?
or did he just let it go!

See the old man ,
at the sidewalk cafe,
watching the passing parade,
just sitting there taking it easy,
he's no longer on the go.

He's the old man ,
at the sidewalk cafe,
living like some Peter Pan,
believing of a better way,
in some never never land.

Oh! he knows his time is fading,
the sunset's kicking in,
he can hear the bell tolling,
is it ringing just for him?
so he sits there taking it in.

See the old man
at the sidewalk cafe,
drinking his coffee neat,
lost in a dream of past glory,
fading so slowly with him.

See the old man,
at the sidewalk cafe,
watching the passing parade,
just sitting there taking it easy,
he's no longer on the go

So he sips his coffee slowly,
forcing a smile once again,
knowing the pain and the pleasure,
are living and dying with him,
so he sits there taking it in.

He knows his days are numbered,
like every man that lives,
knowing the cards he has been dealt,
are living and dying with him,
so he sits there taking it in.

See the old man ,
at the sidewalk cafe,
doing the best that he can,
learning to live,to love and let go,
maybe start over again

Stepping out into the sunshine,
coming in from the road,
living the light and darkness,
starting all over again.

There's an old man,
at the sidewalk cafe,
drinking his coffee slow,
just sitting there taking it easy,
no longer on the go.

See the old man,
at the sidewalk cafe,
watching the passing parade,
just sitting there taking it easy,
he is no longer on the go.

Maybe it's not too late,
the game of patience is the go,
waiting for the hand of fate,
just sitting there taking it easy
with hope for one last deal?

On contemplating Rubens nude.

She came to him alone at night,
a vision of love lost in flight,
he sees her there in the pale moonlight,
a passing flash he once held tight.

She came by lately in the dead of night,
a women of beauty lost in flight,
they shared their love in the pale moonlight,
a moments passion as souls unite

It's then he knew to his great delight,
Rubens got it right ,
Yeah,
Rubens got it right!

Yeah! I'm gazing on a Rubes nude,
a painting on my wall,
remembering our naked kiss,
when you visited my room.

A reminder of a misspent youth,
and the love that's crossed my mind,
when we united in loves embrace,
you were my English rose.

She came by lately on a starry night,
turning his darkness into her light,
painting a picture of music in flight,
all the beauty in colours ran bright.

She came to him by day and by night,
turning his soul from darkness to light,
there in a vision of loves soul insight,
treble and bass in sounds of delight.

It's then he knew to his great delight,
Rubens got it right,
Yeah,
Rubens got it right!

Yeah! I'm gazing on a Rubens nude,
a painting on my wall,
remembering our naked kiss,
when you visited my room.

A reminder of a misspent youth,
and the love that crossed my mind,
when we united in love's embrace,
you were my English rose.

Regaining confidence

Wherever I am that's where I will be,
doing the best that I can,
struggling in weakness to regain strength,
knowing to rest when I will.

Wherever I am that's where I will be,
fighting the pain with compassion,
trying my best to arise into light,
dispelling the darkness I am free.

Wherever I am that's where I will be,
trusting in hope to dispel misery,
doing my best to overcome fear,
sometimes in gladness,often I fear.

Wherever I am that's where I will be,
letting go sadness to bring you joy,
mindful of others before my ploy,
healing through nature and friends.

Wherever I am that's where I will be,
mending ones heart in kindness and truth,
being alone or in a group,
doing the best that i can.

Wherever I am that's where I will be,
building the heart back to youth,
being of service to you,
let what is now written ring true.

CAMINO
WAYS.COM

Section 8- Sarria to Santiago

The relaxing atmosphere of the Rua Maior in Sarria town centre with its fine food,cafes,churches,chapels, monasteries and pilgrim hospitals and a visit to the castle fortress and the Magdalena monastery makes the pilgrims stay a nice respite before the final destination.

The Camino takes the pilgrim through pretty villages and peaceful hamlets under the shade of many old oak trees on quiet country roads.The way passes the beautiful Romanesque church at the village of Barbadelo before crossing the river Mino and a rise uphill towards Serra de Ligonde.

The pilgrim passes the hamlet of Gonzar and Ventas de Naron,the Romanesque churches of Santa Maria in Castromaior and Eirex where a sculpture of Daniel with animals and a pilgrim statue are featured. The trail continues downhill,past village of Casanova steeped in myth and on to the village of Leboreiro and the lively markets of Melide for local octopus,the most classic dish of Galicia.

The Camino crosses several streams and follows a forest track to the village of Boente and its church of Santiago. The medieval village of Ribadisco and the town of Arzua with their churches of Santa Maria and Magdalena are a fitting way to prepare for the final way to Santiago.

The remaining pathway to Santiago takes the pilgrim through woods,sleepy villages and across streams. En route,the unique statue of Santiago and the lovely hamlet of Rua are worth a visit. The rest of the route is a mix of country roads and forest tracks.

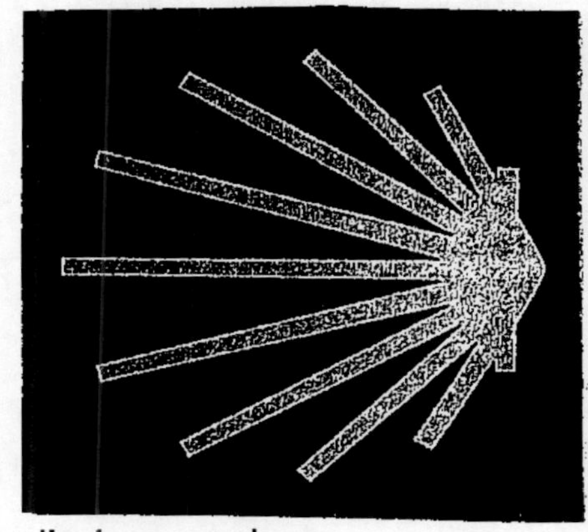

Lavacolla,outskirts of Santiago,is where pilgrims wash in the river in preparation for their arrival in Santiago. Rows of eucalyptus trees line the journey to Monte de Gozo where the pilgrim catches the first glimpse of the cathedral of Santiago.

It is traditional to attend the Pilgrim's Mass at the cathedral,delighting in the stark architecture and the spiritual and cultural Mecca of Santiago.

THE CAMINO DE SANTIAGO-THE EPILOGUE

It was not just journey of the Camino from St-jean-Pied-de-Port to Santiago that led me to my inner call of writing poetry and songs. It was the people I met along the way. Memories of my time in old barque country high in the Pyrenees to the plains of Navarra,the peaks and troughs of the regions of La Rioja,Castilla yLeon,the Meseta region,Cantabrian mountains and the El Bierzo and Galacia and the beauty of cities like Burgos,Leon and Santiago, are all but distant memories,which fade with time.

Sleeping rough and eating the best of pilgrim meals at low cost made the journey interesting also. No, it's the people I met along the way that remain with me. Time with the Irish mother and daughter and stories of the land of my forefathers. The days and evenings spent with the two young Canadian school teachers who, in their spirituality,helped me to come terms with the loss of my son,reintroduced me to prayer and lead me to renew the rituals of the the church of my youth, be that for a brief moment of my Camino. The times with the Danish artist and his son and stories of the ancient viking ways. Laughing with the Dutch kids as we sang on a mountain climb,singing and talking with the two Belgian girls along the track for a day,being poetic with my young German musician friend,eating and drinking with the Greeks,the Italians and the Americans and so many others too numerous to mention.

Notes taken down in haste because I was too busy enjoying the company of new found friends. The odd poem I wrote about those I met along the way are stated here as a gentle reminder of friendships forged My day with the two Spanish beauties recorded here in a poem,the night I sat with the young Korean discussing the damage done by our mothers to our psyche and his plan to kill his mum with a dagger and the repeat dream he was having of a little girl with a dagger in her mouth. All had a lasting impression resulting in the creation of yet another poem.

At the journey led towards its end in Santiago,I wrote some poems more central to where I was at that time from a spiritual and mental state of being.I trust that this final epilogue,is a fitting end and testament to a journey of discovery for you and hopefully further inner growth for both of us,as a result of my Camino.

SANDRO

SECTION 8-THE CAMINO EPILOGUE

DANCING QUEEN.

A BOY NAMED YOUNG.

MISSION WISHING.

ON MY WAY BACK HOME.

WALKING THE CAMINO.

THE BEACH WALK.

THE SCENT OF A ROSE.

LOVE.

LOVE FLOWER ON THE WAY.

DO YOU KNOW THE LOVE.

ITS WHATS WRITTEN IN THE WIND.

UTOPIA.

Dancing queen!

We met each other in a dream,
the night before I met you,
It was like some movie scene,
as you flashed across my mind.

A vision of pure beauty,
you were a dancing queen,
floating to some ancient rhythm,
then you faded away!

I shouted you a coffee,
somewhere along the track,
you smiled and sipped it slowly,
placed your hand upon my lap.

So we walked on together,
smiled and laughed a lot,
sang our fair share of songs,
To beat the blisters and our back pack!

No, we did not talk the same words,
It was signs and signals that,
become a big attraction,
as I straightened up your hat!

We sometimes held each other's hands,
with childlike fun at that,
danced our selves along the way,
The Santiago track!

We parted when in pain and sweat,
I stopped to rest my feet,
drinking warm fresh water,
watched you walk on in the heat!

As fate would have it,
we met again,
later on upon that day,
You cried upon my shoulder,
said goodnight and went to sleep!

I woke early at the albergue,
To start walking before the heat,
passed by your bed,
ruffled your hair,
you smiled yourself to sleep.

A day or two I came upon,
a note in my backpack,
It was written in Spanish,
I did know that,
so I ask a guide to quote.

"Thank you for making me,
a princess on a difficult day,
a kiss for you in friendship,
"Buen Camino,
on your way!"

Sometimes when I cannot sleep,
I think of that fate filled day,
hand in hand with the dancing queen,
was it real or just a mirage,
on the Santiago way.

"We should consider every day lost on which we have not danced at least once."

\- Friedrich Nietzche

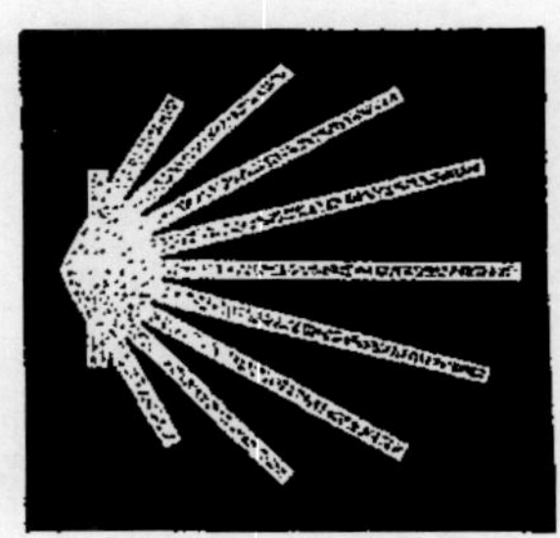

A boy named Young.

Young man in New York City,
in a nightmare dream,
wants to kill his mother,
keeps a dagger right by him.

A little girl with a dagger in her mouth,
in his nightly dreams,
in her eyes the death knell rings,
in her head are warring screams.

New York City,
dark and dirty,
Hudson River,
kinda murky,
sleet is falling
on the ground.

Stock exchange
is closing down,
life is cold,
moon is dead,
blood is fear,
colours red.

New York City,
lost in dreams,
blood stained walls,
the tenement scenes,
shadows fall
on pavement path,
twin towers
vacant gasp .

Young man walks
by the Hudson River,
throws a dagger off the bridge,
he's on his way to Santiago,
with a knapsack on his back.

Young man in his freedom,
back turned to murky waves,
free at last from troubled dreams,
looks to new horizons,
New Yorks a distant haze.

New York City ,
bright and sunny,
Hudson River,
kinda clean,
sun is shining
on the stock exchange
people are running free.

Life is warm,
moon is rising,
blood is love,
colours crimson.

Sun is setting on a monument,
casting light on shadowed land,
twin towers mark the ground,
darkened night was just a dream.

Mother in New York City,
missing her only one,
smiles a song of freedom,
letting go of poison words,
the dagger killing her son.

Young man in a Spanish land,
talks to diamonds in the sky,
a little girl with a dagger
in her mouth,
no longer in his way.

She's fading into darkness,
from whence she come.
She's fading into darkness,
from whence she came.

Oh! Mother,mother,
speak to me now,
soft words
from your ageing lips,
I'm free at last ,
no poison words,
no dagger in my grip.

If only I could see you now,
mother in my dreams.
If only I could see you now,
mother in my dreams.

I pray forgiveness for you,
going back to Santiago!

On My way back home.

My kinfolk taught me how to live,
with gun,sword and knife,
another showed me the dark side,
wine,women and a gambling life.

Still learnt to read the good book,
little good did that book do,
when you have to make a living,
to feed a wife and family .

When she left me in the fall,
I put down my weapons too
gave up the life of drinking,
gambling and wild women.

Now the children have all grown,
grandkids are on the scene,
here I am living out my dream,
when I am not around for them.

Sometimes on a bush track,
other times on the seven seas,
the oceans wide and treacherous,
the lands so dark and mean.

Oh! I trim my sails to the wind,
heading back upstream,
content to walk a mountain track,
on my way to my final home.

Sometimes I hunt for my supper,
occasionally work for bread,
mostly content to abstain to live,
staying in tune with my head.

Well I am doing my own thing,
no longer the old ways,
content to climb a mountain top,
viewing a valley fall below.

It's good to view the flowing waters,
being true to you,
heading back up stream,
paddling my own canoe!

Sitting by still waters,
watching birds in flight,
snakes and arrows no longer,
were silent sounds remain.

When I finally lay down my pack,
put away my canoe,
hand in my driver's licence,
I may just enjoy the view.

Watch the white curls rising,
as I smoke a pipe or two,
sitting on my verandah,
telling stories to grandkids.

Telling stories of the days of yore,
the things that use to be,
see the firelight glisten in small eyes,
with my grandkids on my knee.

In my final prayer,
it will be for you my kin,
not for my mortal soul,
I leave that for the maker then.

So may it be,Amen.

Walking the Camino.

I'm walking the Camino,
on the way to Santiago,
Yea,I'm leaving here today,
'cause I'm on my way,
walking the Camino.

I'm walking the Camino,
on the way to Santiago,
got my knapsack on my back,
heading down the track,
walking the Camino.

Oh!I used to call you honey,
till you spent all my money,
no use looking back,
just heading down the track,
walking the Camino.

Well I had a life of plenty,
until the pile was empty,
wine,women and song,
the pleasures are all gone ,
so,I'm walking the Camino.

No longer chasing pipe dreams,
not afraid to say so,
It is time for giving back,
just contemplating that,
I'm walking the Camino.

I'm walking the Camino,
on the way to Santiago,
no agenda to turn to,
life is what I now do,
walking the Camino.

In the silvery moon I'm dreamy,
cold and wet I'm moody,
with a tear drop in my eye,
just let it all roll bye,
walking the Camino.

Sunny days are friendly,
doing life so easy,
just moving right along,
singing me this song,
walking the Camino.

Well life's a simple fact,
healthy food in my sack,
the rest is giving back,
moving down the track,
walking the Camino.

Walking the Camino,
on the way to Santiago,
Yea,I'm leaving here today,
'cause I'm on my way,
walking the Camino.

Walking the Camino,
on the way to Santiago,
with a knapsack on my back,
just walking down the track,
walking the Camino.

Walking the Camino
on the way to Santiago,
got freedom for a map,
walking the Camino,
on the way to Santiago.

Walking the camino,
on the way to Santiago,
there's just no turning back,
walking the Camino,
on the way to Santiago.

The beach walk.

Oh! The skylark flies across the moon,
on a flamingo painted sky,
heading for its heartland,
high above and alone it flies,
on this Camino way.

Now the curtains drawing back,
to a fiery morning glow,
as the sun also rises,
to a far horizon flow,
on this Camino way.

Rain drops gently falling,
clears the morning air,
and a rainbows leaking colour,
on the canvas of my heart,
on this Camino way.

"Yeah! I was born to wander,
I was born to roam,
you are the pearl in my oyster,
and this world is now my home."

Can you feel it in the sea break,
the gentle lapping of the waves,
the fishermen casting beyond,
in brief of natures gift,
on this Camino way.

There's a man wandering the beach,
another capturing the view,
filming nature's glory,
waves lapping on the sand,
on this Camino way.

The fog is closing in,
distorting the natural view,
and the skylarks returning,
to begin again,
on this Camino way.

"Yeah! I was born to wander,
I was born to roam,
you are the pearl in my oyster,
and this world is now my home."

There are foot prints on the beach,
embedded in the sand,
blended on a timber stairway,
sand is carried there by man,
on this Camino way.

The fog is slowly lifting now,
fishermen are gone,
lone ship on the horizon,
calmly floating home,
on this Camino way.

The sun is bathed in gold,
the sky is crimson red,
the skylark still on the beach,
waiting to be fed,
on this Camino way..

"Yeah! I was born to wander,
I was born to roam,
you are the pearl in my oyster,
and this world is now my home."

There is an old piano,
playing a classic tune,
a melody to fit the mood,
of a man walking the beach alone,
on this Camino way.

The scent of a rose.

So I'm talking to my soul now,
to determine right from wrong,
loving for the right reasons,
sharing with you this song.

It is in the hope and faith now,
faith and loving are so strong,
while you're walking without thought,
you can sing this song.

"So I'm walking the road less travelled,
once more in fields of clover,
moving from darkness to light.
handing over the thorn in my heart,
for the smell of the scent of a rose!"

Oh! know I am in a world waiting,
in a heart that's no longer afraid,
living from moment to moment,
walking my Camino way.

There is a smile in my sunlight,
listening to the nightingale,
the Master is inside me waiting,
for the sacred word to come.

Yeah! I am living moment to moment,
breathing in the vibrating earth,
waiting for the great exposition,
creations word between heaven and earth.

"So I'm walking the road less travelled,
once more in a field of clover,
moving from darkness to light,
handing over the thorn in my heart,
for the smell of the scent of a rose."

Letting go of the child within me,
coming to a new rebirth,
no longer listening to the carrion crow,
it's now the God of the universe.

Just to be where you're standing,
on a mountain or valley floor,
content to be in a crowd or alone,
time with the rich and the poor.

"So I'm walking the road less travelled ,
once more in a field of clover,
moving from darkness to light,
handing over the thorn in my heart,
for the smell of the scent of a rose."

You have so much to give my friend,
we have so much that we know,
it's all in the silent moment,
we've just got to let it show.

The plant germinates in the soil,
goes through so much pain to grow,
breaking through the earth like a baby at birth,
to the lotus flower that we all know.

So go deep inside my friend,
to germinate your flower,
you have so much to give back now,
you've just got to let it grow.

"So I'm walking the road less travelled ,
once more in a field of clover,
moving from darkness to light,
handing over the thorn in my heart,
for the smell of the scent of a rose."

Love.

Is it the sound I'm hearing in the trees,
do I see you in the falling leaves,
maybe it's the sweetness of the breeze,
the feel of sand between my toes.

We did our mating in some distant past,
life was always splendid in the grass,
now feelings are faded memories,
and nothing ever lasts for long.

Is it the woman cradled in my arms,
the warmth of her constant charms,
maybe it's the child upon my lap,
that sense of innocence.

Oh! Love,
come back into my room,
and take away these blues.

Did I see you in the corner of my eye,
the shadow of the bird flying by,
the warmth of the sun upon my face,
maybe now in a fading cloud.

Do I see you in the smiling faces,
the parade of the human races,
maybe it's in some isolation ,
on some foreign plain.

Did I see you somewhere on the road,
was it a gentle hand upon my back,
maybe it's the burden of the load,
when I am looking back.

Oh! Love
come back into my room,
and take away my blues.

Are you there with the man in the moon,
did I see you in a shooting star,
the flash of light in star studded sky,
that faded out too soon.

Is it true you were here at the start,
maybe back there in my mother's womb,
were are you now my gentle one,
is it because I am lost and worn?

Now I am here out upon the track,
walking with my knapsack on my back,
taking the rough with the smooth,
looking for the love that I once knew.

Oh! love,
come back into my room,
and take away these blues.

Yesterday we did cartwheels on high,
laughed a lot until we said goodbye,
and the wheel is still in spin,
hoping you'll return again.

We came together staring into space,
listened to the sound between the chords,
danced our way together in the rain,
then we just died in tune.

Now I'm here out upon the track,
walking with my knapsack on my back,
taking the rough with the smooth,
looking for the love that I once knew.

Oh! Love ,
come back into my room,
and take away these blues.

Love flower on the way.

You are the flower,
that springs from the womb,
of the dark earth's power,
once a seed entombed.

In sunlight or shadow,
you continue to bloom,
your radiance blossoms,
so I sing you love's tune.

To love's flower,my heart's burning,
with flaming love for you,
my heart with wanderlust-yearning,
shall tramp this heavenly course.

Fellow pilgrims walk along,
singing with loudest song,
it is in my heart sun flower,
in every hearth loves home.

So keep the logs on the fire,
watch the embers glow.
as I warm myself by evening,
It's your love I long to hold.

As the embers cool by morning,
I face the rising sun,
with a knapsack and tucker bag,
winding my way back home.

To love's flower,my hearts burning,
with flaming love for you,
my heart with wanderlust-yearning,
shall tramp this heavenly course.

Fellow pilgrims walk along,
singing with loudest song,
it is in my heart sun flower,
in every hearth and home.

So we tramp this path together,
and we tramp this path alone,
touched by the beauty of the flower
the sun flower for me,the rose.

Oh! love's been touched by flower,
and heart's been torn by the thorns,
in this earthly hour ,
I sing love's beauty ,this song.

Whilst pilgrims walk along,
singing this loudest song,
the sacred heart,rose flower,
you are in my heart,my home.

The hearth with dying embers,
breath life into the fire,
give your heart to love eternal,
help me to feed the flame.

To love's flower,my hearts burning,
with flaming love for you,
my heart with wanderlust-yearning,
shall tramp this heavenly course.

Wild roses bloom in wilderness,
thorns are hidden from view,
this heart in the morning glow,
reveals my love for you.

Tramping this track along,
blessed be with loudest song,
whilst embers die by morning,
my love will see me through.

The flame will keep on burning,
in every hearth love's song,
the flame will keep on burning,
in every heart loves home.

Do you know the love.

Baby,is it the love
that keeps me grounded,
the feelings in my heart,
that state of mind?

Oh! I can't tell you lies,
I've got no reason,
got too much sense of pain,
and too much pride.

The singer tells in song,
to hide your feelings,
its never worked for me,
it never will.

So I'll just say it here
with pure emotion,
what's going on in me,
is going on in you.

"Just cry out loud,
don't keep it inside,
learn how to share,
your feelings.

Sing wild and proud,
make life a song,
just try to share,
your feelings."

Is it because I forgot,
to bring you flowers,
maybe I missed,
our dinner date.

Maybe it's because
I am feeling lonely,
need some time,
just to contemplate.

Don't misunderstand,
it's not about you,
my absent mindedness,
my love for you.

"Just cry out loud,
don't keep it inside,
learn how to share ,
your feelings.

Sing wild and free,
make life a song,
just try to share,
your feelings."

Baby,know that in
your waiting,
I do understand,
your point of view.

Love is not a gift,
wrapped and labelled,
a word put on a card,
it's in the heart.

It can't be bottled up,
like a brand of wine,
taken off the shelf,
when it is matured.

Drink of the cup,
the pain of wine and roses,
love is like that,
an ever flowing dream.

"Just cry out loud,
don't keep it inside,
learn how to share,
your feelings.

Sing wild and free,
make life a song,
just try to share ,
your feelings.

Fly high and proud,
and remember,
we must let go,
to love."

It's what's written in the wind.

There's sunshine in the darkness,
a twinkle in your eye,
wandering down some strange road,
the feelings in your lonely heart,
are here with you once more,
It's what's written in the wind.

Especially when the westerly wind,
comes blowing at your door,
then all your senses are attuned,
as you lean into the breeze,
no comfort to a wandering heart,
It's what's written in the wind.

It's not always easy,
when you're living nature's way,
doing your best now,
to let go your load,
searching for freedom,
on your Camino road,
on your Camino road.

Tramping down a lonely road,
lost and alone upon this path,
no comfort in the searching,
winging a way back to you,
It's always been your destiny,
It's what's written in the wind.

Guess you know the answer,
cease the valleys,hills and dale,
give up the quest out on the track,
knock upon her door once more,
let your heart return to home,
It's what's written in the wind.

It's not always easy,
when your living nature's way,
doing your best now,
to let go your load,
searching for freedom,
on your Camino road,
on your Camino road.

Everything you're searching for,
it's already within you,
let your feet do the walking,
keep the dream alive,
walking with hearts drum beat,
it's what's written in the wind.

There's sunshine in the darkness,
a twinkle in your eye,
wandering down a strange land,
touched by a moonbeam on high,
the feelings in your lonely heart,
It's what's written in the wind.

It's not always easy,
when your living nature's way,
doing your best now,
to let go your load,
searching for freedom,
on your Camino road,
on your Camino road.

Distant heart hears the drum,
wounds of love are bitter sweet,
feet are tramping to a sound,
call of the wild is your heart beat,
It's what's written in the wind.

It's not just your heart now,
it's the song within you,
the voice of her heart calling,
the call is just for you,
is it the call of the wild,
It's whats' written in the wind.

It's not always easy,
when your living nature's way,
doing your best now,
to let go your load,
searching for freedom,
on your Camino road,
on your Camino road.

Searching for freedom,
on your Camino road,
Searching for freedom,
on your Camino road,
it's the call of the wild,
it's what's written in the wind.

Utopia.

Walking on this mystic path,
seeing the sun set in a violet sky,
passing signposts along the way,
a gateway to my destiny,
good karma's is on high.

Reflecting on dreams to come,
learning from the past,
feeling the presence on the way,
listening to inner sounds,
destiny on firm ground.

It's the oneness of being,
in the newness of time,
letting go of emotional baggage,
heading to Utopia,
heading to Utopia,

Oh!you know the way of the spirit,
time and energy in your stride,
keep the spirit of your mindset,
and true pilgrims by your side,
living in the moment of Utopia.

The lesson of the Camino.
to clear old karma,
reset the souls direction,
on a track less travelled by,
a way to reincarnation,
heading to Utopia.

There is light upon the pathway,
good karma in your stride,
meditating in the moment,
the mindfulness is the way,
heading for my shelter,Utopia.

The planets are aligned,
the days are warm and sunny,
night skies are diamond starlight,
there is magic in your eyes,
when you get Utopia.

Oh! You know the way of the spirit,
time and energy in your stride,
keep the spirit of your mindset,
and true pilgrims by your side,
living in the moment of Utopia.

" I said to my soul,be still,and wait without hope
for hope would be hope for the wrong thing;
wait without love
For love would be love of the wrong thing;
there is yet faith
But the faith and the love and the hope
are all in the waiting.
Wait without thought,for you are not
ready for thought:
So the darkness shall be the light,
and the stillness the dancing."

T.S.Eliot,'East Coker',Four Quartets.

He had arrived as the dawn broke over the city of Santiago.The early morning rays shone over the Cathedral steeples in the heart of a sea of grey building,silhouettes emerging from the darkness.The constant pounding of his feet on the cobble stones in tune with the beat of his heart,a heart that was beating to the tune of his own drummer. On arrival at the Praza de Obradoiro,the large open plaza outside the Cathedral,he was greeted and hugged by so many of his fellow pilgrims whom he had met along the way.He felt like he was with a silent but loving group of angels and he was entering a seventh heaven.He felt the presence of medieval pilgrims who had gathered here and kept vigil in the plaza so many centuries ago.

The Cathedral was packed with two thousand pilgrims for the midday Sunday service where the spectacle of the Botafumeiro ,the "smoke belcher"swung back and forth from a pulley of ropes by eight men.He remembered it was installed in the medieval days to cover the stench of all the unwashed pilgrims during the mass for pilgrims.On this day,as in ever modern spiritual service,the botafumeiro with the sweet smell of incense spreading smoke,was to him a symbol to cleanse the world of darkness, cleanse the souls of man that the many pilgrims present from all over the world here represented. The camino had cleanse his own soul from darkness into a light to live,really live.

He walked the few blocks from the Cathedral to the pilgrim's office and waited in line with his fellow pilgrims to receive his Compostela,the document of completion awarded to those of us who had walked the Camino way to Santiago.He produced his Credential,the pilgrims passport identifying him as a pilgrim,with proof stamps of accommodation and sites he had visited along the way.He for a brief moment thought of his childhood and felt like he had just received his confirmation once more being a soldier of Christ like the great soldier of Spain,St James, the Greater.

He spent the afternoon wandering in a semi daze ,enjoying the laughter,love and conversation with his small band of brothers and sister of the Camino .Those special souls he had met and spent time with alone and in groups ,along the way.He knew something about the heart of each of them and they too knew something about his heart.They all met that Sunday evening for a last supper together.He was weary and feeling a sense of foreboding of the farewell to follow.He hugged each of them in turn,and like them,promised that they would meet again some day and he walked away into the night,led by the light of the street lamps ,back to his hotel room.

He awoke the next morning and wandered the city alone ,but greeted by many other pilgrims just arriving and whom he had met along the way.He ventured back to the Cathedral as it was early morning and the cathedral was relatively empty.He followed the ancient ritual and climbed the small stairs to touch the golden statue of Santiago, the statue of St.James.In keeping with tradition,he gave the statue a hug but could not bring himself to say prayers of thanks,as is a custom.He descended to the crypt,below the statue where the bones of St.James and his two followers are reported to be buried.

He found himself on both knees on a nearby pew saying a prayer of guidance. He,in truth, knew the bones had been misplaced for almost 300 years before being returned to the Cathedral in the sixteenth century and there was no real proof that they were the bones of the saint in any case.He once more walked the city in search of a symbol of his quest to Santiago.Yes,he had laid down so many inner burdens and walked the traditional way of so many pilgrims before him.He was searching for the fulfilment of a myth,a symbolic Sword of Discernment,the sword of St James ,the disciple of Christ, who probably never walked on Spanish soil in his life,never mounted a steed and never led a great charge against the Moors.The facts disproved the myth,but the myth remains and many other pilgrims through the centuries have ventured on the pathway to Santiago in search of their own heart's desires,in letting go,in healing,in companionship,in a spiritual quest or just to take a long walk.

Fact or fiction,the story remains and the journey is real for each pilgrim who takes to the road and let the feet do the walking.The realisation that his search was in vain, he found his way to the market place and purchased gifts for friends and family as memento of his Compostela.So determined to return to Australia with some symbol of his Sword of Discernment,he settled for a black shirt with a red sword of the Knights Templar on the front.The sacrificial cross of St.James,a floury Fitch,where the sword blade makes it the sword of a warrior.

He was not to realise at that time that the seed of his creativity was in the heart of a lotus flower,a flower that was nestled in his heart which would spring forth from the mouth of the dark dragon that lay dead with the sword that had pieced its heart,in his heart of hearts.The seed that would spring into creative verse,song and books he would write and sing as a result of his Camino journey.A seed that would see his return to the journey of the way for him.

Yes, he would walk the Camino de Santiago again and he would produce a Sword of Discernment, but it would be a pen that would prove to him mightier than the sword.It would be the creative expression in words he would write and songs he would sing that would be his Sword of Discernment.It would be the love that would come to him like a Christ walking on the fragments of stone that ventured toward him on pierced feet.

The Myth and the reality.

He had emerged from the darkness into the light,like a knight of old,he had exhausted many talents though pursuing many causes and ideals that were not of his standard.He had fought the good fight for noble causes,lofty goals,laurel wreaths that in the end proved fruitless.Nothing rust so quickly as an unused sword or a soldier with nothing to do.He had achieved the desires of his worldly quests so many times before and now he was like a tiger without a prey,restless,irritable and discontented.The Camino had been a great relief to what had ailed him for so long.The loss of wife,son,family ,business and ultimately health issues had culminated into a journey inward that had been long overdue.He no longer had to suffer all the pain and hunger,weariness and discipline of the past.He had achieved an outer peace yet there was no peace within.It was not the peace of those destined for war that he most craved.It was the outward expression of something immeasurably larger than his former self to which he must now turn.

He realised in his contemplation,that in order to renew a commitment to life and discover a future full of potential,he must find a new goal;but this new goal would need to be much bigger than his personal aspirations.He had already fulfilled his personal ambitions and some of the fruit of the vine of his dreams and aspirations had withered on the vine.He knew it was his fatherly duty to do his best to provide water to keep the tree of life,of which he was partly too, alive.Other than that,he had turned within to discover what it had all been for and now it was time to nurture the seed that was within his creative imagination,to grow a new tree for a greater whole, in order to ,in some small way,allow life to flow within again.

He had slain the mythical dragon that had held him captive in his headlong rush in empire building.The initial quest was to rebuild the mansions of material wants that had cracked and crumbled during the supremacy of his inner dragon.However,he soon came to realise that his former striving no longer held weight with him .So he turned to the king of wisdom within and he saw,in his vision,the workings of the bees.How they toiled for the queen ,produced the nectar that had sustained life in time immemorial. Mankind throughout the history of the universe has strived for the leader,for independence,for peace, for understanding,for wealth,for power for land only to see it all crumble and start all over again.The bees continued to collect the nectar died ,as did the queen bee and were replaced by their offspring to repeat the process over again.

He thought of the Hindu parable of Indra and the parade of ants.How Indra,the God of thunder,lightning and earth,flung his thunderbolt into the midst of the ungainly coils, and the dragon monster shattered like a stack of withered rushes.The dragon that had held all the heavenly waters captive in its belly was cut open.Then,the waters broke free and streamed across the land,to circulate once more the body of the earth.It was then that the Gods of the heavens returned to the summit of the mountain and reigned from on high.It was then all the divinities of heaven acclaimed Indra their saviour and greatly elated his triumph.So the mighty Indra summoned the God of arts and crafts,to erect a palace to befit his unequalled splendour.So the work progressed and Indra's demands grew more exacting and his vision vast. Vishvakarman,The divine craftsmen, the maker of all, built pavilions,ponds,groves and pleasure grounds all to the will of Indra.The work finally brought the craftsmen to despair and he turned to the great creator God Brahma who ordered him to go home in peace for he would soon be relieved of his burden.

Brahma then went to seek Vishnu,the Supreme being,whom Brahma himself was but an agent.Vishnu in turn let it be known that Vishvakarman's request would be fulfilled.

Early the next morning,a small boy carrying the staff of a pilgrim appeared at the gate of Indra.The king of the Gods bowed to the holy child,for he saw the radiance of the his wisdom.Indra enquired of the purpose of the child's visit.The child enquired of the years it would take to fulfil Indra palace dream to completion and what further nobel feats would be required of Vishvakarman to perform.Indra,in his lofty pride,enquired how many Indra he, the child had seen or heard of,in his short life.

The child replied that he had indeed seen many.He knew his father,the old tortoise man,his grandfather,the beam of celestial light, the son of Brahma and he knew Vishu,the Supreme Being and he had seen and known the dreadful dissolution of the universe.He stated that he had seen all perish,again and again,at the end of every cycle.At which time every single atom dissolved into pure waters of eternity,whence everything originally arose and he questioned the Indra "who can count the universes that have passed away or the creations that have risen afresh from the formless abyss of the waters?Who will number the passing ages of the world?and who will search through the wide infinities of space to count the universes side by side,each with its Brahma and its Vishnu?Who will count the Indra in them all,ascending to godly kingship one by one,and one by one pass away?

Then the boy began to laugh,for the boy caught sight of a parade of ants as in military array,they moved across the earth.The Indra enquired of his laughter and he replied "I laugh because of the secret of the ants."The Indra asked for some sign of the revelation of the secret and the boy responded "I saw the ants,each one an Indra, ascending to the rank of a king of the gods.But now,through many rebirths,each has again become an ant.Piety and high deeds elevate living beings to the glorious realm of celestial mansions.But wicked acts sink them into the worlds beneath,into the pits of pain and sorrow.It is by deeds that one merits happiness or anguish,and becomes master or servant.This is the whole substance of the secret,life is a cycle of countless rebirths and is like a vision in a dream.The gods,the trees,the stones are like apparitions in this fantasy. But death administers the law of time and is the master of all.Hence the wise are attached to neither good nor evil.The wise are not attached to anything at all."

Then an old hermit appeared between Indra and the boy and sat upon the floor in meditation.The boy enquired of the man's name and purpose,of which the old man,still in a state of mindfulness,replied that his name was 'Hairy'.He stated he had a short time to live and had no worldly possessions,had no wife,no children and had no desire to work. He stated that he existed by begging alms and he grew hair long to teach wisdom and as each Indra fell,he lost one hair.That is why he was bald ,but grew a beard and chest hair and stated that when the present Indra had gone,he too would die.He exclaimed what use was there of a wife, children, a house ,if ,in the flicking of a eyelid of the Supreme Being,a Brahma passes and everything else is but a cloud taking shape and again dissolving.The old man summed up by stating ,he did not crave to experience the various blissful forms of redemption but to devote himself to meditating on the incompatible feet of the highest Vishnu.

Abruptly,the holy old hermit and the boy vanished and the king Indra was alone baffled and amazed.He wondered if it had been a dream but no longer felt any wish to magnify his heavenly splendour.He summoned Visvakarman and heaped gifts upon him,then sent the craftsman -god home.Indra now desired redemption for he had acquired

Wisdom and longed to be free.He resolved to retire to the hermit life and leave the burden of his office to his children.But the call of his resolve was diverted by the Lord of Magic wisdom.The Lord spoke of the virtues of the spiritual life,the virtues of the secular and gave to each its due.Indra relented and was restored to a joyful state. He fulfilled that which he had been created to do in the transient universe of which he was a part,and no longer feared or felt enraged about the parade of ants,or the Indra's past and to come.

So he ,who had tramped the Camino, awoke from the vision of the Indra and the parade of ants.He thought of the duty of the bees in their collection of nectar ,the devotion to the queen and the magic of the creation of honey.He thought of how even the king of the Gods had been humbled and brought to the knowledge of his proper role in the great play of unending life.He thought of the wisdom of living a balanced life,mindful of both body and spirit,of being content to be unique.Of the fact that being great or small,human or ant,God or human,was just a spark of life,a part of a vast living unity whose intentions and workings are orderly and yet beyond man's grasp.

He could see he had done his share of building palaces,seeking knowledge of creating wealth,and power and of providing for wife and family.It was their turn now,his children and grandchildren.He would be there,but only as a guide to point the way through,for whatever purpose unfolded for him ,if they indeed sought his help.He had done more than his fair share of serving his all and his community, but he had done it all for lofty goals in a service of mythical belief,in fulfilling a dream that had died with the breakdown of all that he had created.It was time to rebuild in a new way, a new goal,a renewal of servitude that would be done more gently,with less individual purpose and more in keeping with a balanced life for his own and community.

He had suffered so much in his transition to this new state of being and was beginning to accept things as they are ,as he let go the old and embraced the newThe contemplation of his past,the Indra myth and the journey of the Camino was leading him to a new light to guide him.Whilst he was aware of a unique purpose to fulfil his destiny,he knew he had to keep things in perspective.His worldly duties would continue,his Sword of Discernment would unfold in time,but he would remember the never ending working of the bees ,he would remember the parade of ants.Ahead he saw a guiding light,a vision of great splendour ,a light that transmitted to him a vision for the future,a light that he was mindful,not to be blinded by.

He was walking out of the darkness into the light.

AUTHOR'S ACKNOWLEDGMENTS

The practice of pilgrimage has been the chosen experience of thousands of people who have taken a path less travelled for centuries.The experience of walking historic,religious and spiritual sites all over the world has had a resurgence in the 21st century. The Camino de Santiago has become the benchmark for many who are on a search meaning,direction and vision for their future or who just want to experience something different. The Camino for me was a catalyst to my renewed yearning for adventure and a turning point in my choice of lifestyle for the future.

The poetry of this book and the songs that have since been written and recorded would not have eventuated in the form that they have ,if it was not for my Camino pilgrimage. So many pathways treversed and many new friendships forged. The greetings and blessings inspirited much creative output as a result of the journey.Special thanks to my pilgrim friends along the way,Jacinta and Vanessa from Ireland ,Julie and Nicole, Canada, Chon and Francois France and Alain from Sydney. Robin from Germany for his brotherly love and musical inspiration, Dan,Czech Republic, for in-depth conversation,Young from New York and Roland from Germany. Nino and his daughter Lauren for Spanish translation and help at critical moments on my journey.Raphael and his great stories and fitness tips.The Greeks, Vangelis and Lefteris ,Guavas,the medical man,Juana and Alejandra,the Spanish beauties for a happy day on the road,Nicole for her free spirit and happy conversations.

Sing -a -longs with Jane and the inspiration of Christa,the retired German ballet teacher. Marien and her fellow companion Nadine from Belgium,for the laughter and songs as we climbed the mountain tracks together. The Dutch students with whom I sang my merry way over hill and dale. Raimon for his kind ways,Sandy for his friendship and attention to detail in the Albergue at Burgos. Brother John of the order of the brothers of Mother Theresa for his friendly words and prayer. Conversations with Aaron,Karl and Peter from Austria,Julia from Germany, Stephanie from Canada,Domenico and Mikko from Italy Anne Marie from down town New York for enthusiasm and her welcome on arrival in Santiago. John and Jill,David and Anne ,Will and Alice all from U.K. Jordi, Aurelie and Warfus from Austria and so many others,too numerous to mention here. All had a profound influence on my journey of the spirit and for this ,apart from the friendships forged,I am most grateful.

A special thanks to Franki Pollick for photographic work for the cover of this book, the reproduction of the painting by awarding winning artist Sandra Lalopoulos in the garden scene. David Milling and Zoe Blockley for draft copies and printing and Peter Thorpe for website graphics and text. Special thanks to those whose inspirational words of the mythic journey inspired me to write on myth, for their insight of the meaning of myth has afforded me some poetic licence in a guide to my life and journal on the Camino way.

"We all know the gutter,
but some of us are looking at the stars."

-Oscar Wilde

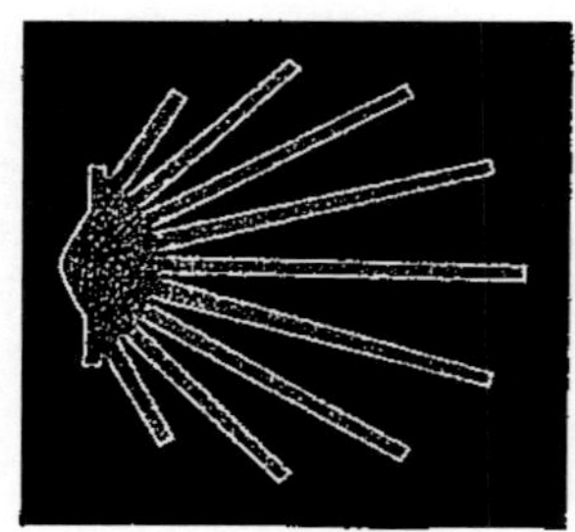

Afterthoughts:

As I close this final chapter to this content of memories of my poems, thoughts and documented philosophies of my trek on the Camino de Santiago,I am reminded of the facts of the reality of my existence and not the words upon a page. In piecing together poems from my note book and photos from my little phone and the rough notes in my journal to write this book,it became for me another Camino,reliving the Way once again. Although it was not the same physical effort of walking The Way,it was a journey to to the same end.

It was not without its mishaps,as I lost my computer records that could have made my task much easier to transcribe. Instead,I have had to depend upon hardcopy that I had kept in case of further mishaps and it is those that I have use here rather than do a rewrite.It is no easy task to convert hardcopy to a pdf file and then convert it to a word document. Whilst,this action in fact was attempted,the result was not so good ,so I settled for copy and print of my hardcopy notes.

So,whilst my formatting of this document is not professional,it does serve its purpose as a readable account of my search for meaning and soul searching on my Camino.I trust that you accept this account of one who may be a bit of wordsmith but lacks the skills of IT computing and format.

This poetic journal has not had the scrutiny of my novel,which is in proof read as I write. Whilst I may sometimes loose the plot with spelling and punctuation,I trust more than the rough nature of the layout of these pages that you gain some small benefit from this my journal of the soul.

In my past depressed state of mind before my Camino,I read daily reflections from a little book called "God Calling." They were a road map back to health for me at that time. The words in that book were a God send and part of the road map back to health that still resonate to this day. In the inside front cover I had written some notes for my daily routine.

"Trust in the slow work of God. Smile and greet,offer assistance. Do nice things for others and keep it to yourself. Listen to others,be patient and wait. Allow others the glory and surrender your need.Live in the present and your efforts will pay dividends. Imagine everyone else is enlightened except you. Do I want to be happy or right? Be patient and open hearted in the moment and you will receive your just reward."

Trust you are living your dream and thank you for sharing my journey of the Spirit and happy tramping until we meet again.

Doug McPhillips

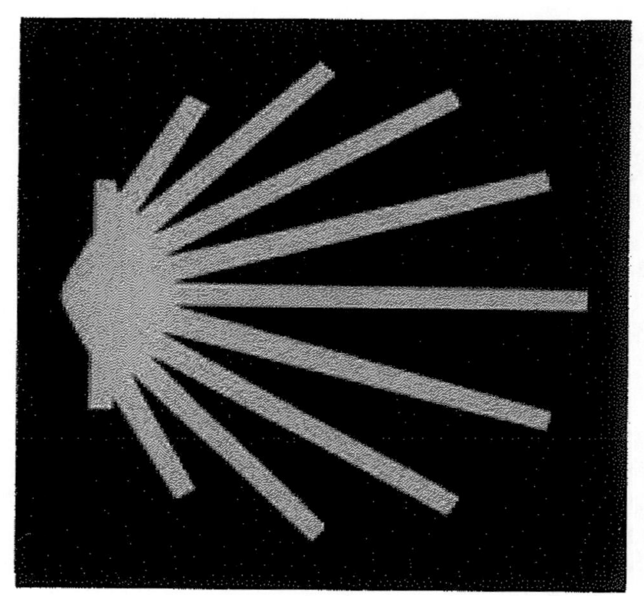